AF835385

29.

03. FEB 95

MAY 95

18. SEP 95

27. SEP 97

DISCARDED

SPRINGFIELD

KENT
COUNTY
LIBRARY

CRANSTON, R
1992: the legal
implications

Books should be returned or renewed by the last date stamped above.

C150598405

1992:
THE LEGAL IMPLICATIONS FOR BANKING

1992: THE LEGAL IMPLICATIONS FOR BANKING

Edited by Ross Cranston

The Chartered Institute of Bankers

Centre for Commercial Law Studies
Queen Mary College · University of London

C150598405
346.08

First Published 1989

Apart from any fair dealing for the purposes of research or private study, or criticism or review, as permitted under the Copyright, Designs and Patents Act 1988, this publication may only be reproduced, stored or transmitted, in any form or by any means, with the prior permission in writing of the publishers, or in the case of reprographic reproduction in accordance with the terms of licences issued by the Copyright Licensing Agency. Enquiries concerning reproduction outside those terms should be sent to the publishers at the undermentioned address:

BANKERS BOOKS LIMITED
c/o The Chartered Institute of Bankers
10 Lombard Street
London EC3V 9AS

Chartered Institute of Bankers (CIB) Publications are published by Bankers Books Ltd under an exclusive licence and royalty agreement. Bankers Books Ltd is a company owned by The Chartered Institute of Bankers.

© The Chartered Institute of Bankers 1989 and Centre for Commercial Law Studies, Queen Mary College, University of London.

British Library Cataloguing in Publication Data

1992: The Legal Implications for Banking (Banking law seminar).
1. International banking. Law
I. Cranston, Ross II. Chartered Institute of Bankers
III. Series 342.6′8215

ISBN 0 85297 243 1

Typeset in 10/11 pt Times Roman by Kerrypress Ltd, Luton, Beds
Text printed on 115 gsm Nimrod High Bulk
Printed and bound by Hartnolls Ltd, Bodmin, Cornwall

CONTENTS

TABLE OF EUROPEAN COMMUNITY TREATIES

TABLE OF EUROPEAN COMMUNITY SECONDARY LEGISLATION

Directives

Regulations

TABLE OF UK STATUTES

TABLE OF CASES

THE CONTRIBUTORS

Ross Cranston — Sir John Lubbock Professor of Banking Law and Dean of the Faculty of Laws, Queen Mary College, University of London.

Marc Dassesse — Professor of EEC Tax Law, Institute of European Studies, Brussels University; De Smedt & Dassesse, Brussels.

Michael Fowle — Senior Banking and Finance Partner, Peat Marwick McLintock, London.

Roy Goode — Crowther Professor of Credit and Commercial Law and Director of Centre for Commercial Law Studies, Queen Mary College, University of London.

Robert R Pennington — Professor of Commercial Law, University of Birmingham.

Paul Tillett — Deputy Secretary, British Bankers' Association, London.

John A Usher — Professor of European Law and Dean of the Faculty of Law, University of Exeter.

PREFACE

Now in their seventh year, the banking law seminars, organised jointly by The Chartered Institute of Bankers and the Centre for Commercial Law Studies at Queen Mary College, University of London, need no introduction to those interested in the subject. Nor does the importance of the present seminar on the banking implications of 1992 need underlining. The single internal market, and the many directives to implement this, will have significant implications for banking and finance.

The papers on which this book is based benefited greatly from expert commentaries by William Blair, barrister, London; Richard Calnan, solicitor and partner, Norton Rose, London; Professor Walter van Gervan, Advocate-General, European Court of Justice, formerly Belgian Banking Commissioner; Dr Mann CBE, FBA, solicitor and consultant, Herbert Smith & Co., London; Dr Hannes Schneider, lawyer and notary, Mueller Weitzel Weisner, Frankfurt; Nick Segal, solicitor and partner, Allen & Overy; and Walter Simpson, Director, Strategic Planning, Girobank.

Acknowledgements should also be made to Mary Lewis, of The Chartered Institute of Bankers, who organised the seminar superbly and Uschi Gubser, who very effectively guided the papers to early publication.

This was the first of the seminars not organised by Alan Miller of The Chartered Institute of Bankers. Their success has derived greatly from his quiet, but effective, organisational skills, wise advice, and gentle prodding of the seminars' academic directors. I am sure that they will continue in the same vein under Mary Lewis' guidance.

The proposal for a Second Banking Directive of February 1988, which formed the basis of discussion at the banking law seminar, appears as an Appendix to this book. Since then, the Council of Ministers agreed to some amendments which are not incorporated in this publication.

1—1992 AND THE IMPLICATIONS FOR BANKING AND FINANCE: AN OVERVIEW

John A Usher

Without denying the psychological importance of the date 1992 in arousing a general awareness of Community law, the rules of the EEC Treaty relevant to the activities of financial institutions remain those which have been in force since the end of the transitional period, subject to certain procedural amendments. Hence, this chapter is largely concerned with Community law and banking and finance rather than with 1992 and banking and finance. What does, however, appear to have changed is the political willingness to give effect to those rules, and financial services are considered in some detail in the White Paper on completing the internal market. In Lord Cockfield's White Paper, emphasis is put on the free circulation of 'financial products', with the suggestion that a similar approach could be taken to that adopted with regard to the free movement of goods. When such an analogy was in fact pursued by the European Court at the end of 1986, the result, as will be seen, was not perhaps what the Commission expected or desired. Might it be suggested that the term 'financial products', although used in UK financial service legislation, is not very helpful. It seems to imply that financial services may be equated with goods which can simply be bought and taken away, whereas the fundamental problem with financial services in European Community law is that what is on offer is a continuing legal relationship, the very nature of which may be dependent upon the local legal system.

In reality, financial services are a matter of particular complexity in the context of the EEC Treaty because they link the provisions specifically relating to movements of money, in particular the movement of capital (arts. 67 to 73) and current payments (art. 106), to the general provisions concerning establishment, services and competition, even if in the view of the European Court, a clear distinction may be drawn between 'means of payment' and goods, so that means of payment do not benefit from the principle of the free movement of goods.[1] They also raise the awkward political question, going beyond a basic consideration of the legal texts, as to whether in fact an integrated market for financial services or for the movement of capital can in reality be achieved without a form of control of currency fluctuations between the exchange rates of the currencies of Member States. Or, indeed, without the development of common currency units, a question which obviously involves consideration of the scope and membership of the European Monetary System[2] and the use of European Currency Units.[3]

However, the aim of this chapter is to deal initially with the general and well-known provisions on establishment, services and competition as they affect financial services, before moving to the special rules which relate to money.

ESTABLISHMENT

Quite apart from the general rules on freedom of establishment, it is worth noting that in the original form of the Treaty there were restrictive provisions with regard to certain aspects of the establishment of financial institutions. The second paragraph of art. 57, as originally drafted, required the Council to act by unanimity on measures concerned with the protection of savings, in particular the granting of credit and the exercise of the banking profession. One of the more positive results of the Single European Act is that by virtue of arts. 6 and 16 of that Act, this special provision with regard to the protection of savings etc, has been deleted and it would appear that this is now an area where the Council is to act by a qualified majority in co-operation with the European Parliament.

Establishment as defined in art. 52 of the Treaty includes the setting-up of agencies, branches, or subsidiaries and the right to set up and manage undertakings, in particular companies or firms within the meaning of art. 58(2). In the light of this, and providing a first link with the monetary provisions of Community law, it is worth noting that from the outset the directives on the movement

1. *R* v *Thompson*, Case 7/78 [1978] ECR 2247. In so far as the European Court treated Krugerrands in that case as being the subject of monetary transfer falling outside the free movement of goods, it has been heavily criticised – see F.A. Mann, *Legal Aspects of Money*, 4th ed., 1982, pp. 24–5.
2. Created by the Resolution of the European Council of 5 December 1978 (EC Bulletin 1978 No. 12 Point 1.1.11) and EC Council Regulation 3181/78 (OJ 1978 L379/2).
3. Defined by Council Regulation 3180/78 (OJ 1978 L379/1) as amended by Council Regulation 2626/84 (OJ 1984 L247/1).

of capital[4] have required Member States to permit direct investments.[5] Direct investments are defined[6] as relating to the establishment and extension of branches of new undertakings belonging solely to the person providing the capital, and the acquisition in full of existing undertakings, or participation in new or existing undertakings with a view to establishing or maintaining lasting economic links, and also include reinvestment of profits with a view to maintaining lasting economic links.

Traditionally in this area of the law, the European Court has been rather reluctant to make a clear distinction between establishment and services.[7] However, in the recent insurance cases,[8] the court has endeavoured to make a clear distinction between establishment and services, holding that if an undertaking is established in another Member State, even by means of a branch or permanent agency, it may not invoke the provisions relating to services. Whilst this may be justifiable on a literal interpretation of the provisions relating to services, which define services in effect as economic activities that do not fall within the other freedoms,[9] it is hardly the type of interpretation which one has learnt to expect from the European Court of Justice.[10] This judgment appears to have influenced the drafting of Council Directive 88/357,[11] the Second Insurance Directive, art. 3 of which in effect deems any permanent presence, including a mere office managed by the undertaking's own staff or by a person who is independent but has permanent authority to act for the undertaking, as establishment, but art. 13 of which requires that undertakings established in a Member State should be allowed to cover certain risks by way of provision of services. However, whatever form

4. Council Directive of 11 May 1960 (JO 1960 p. 921), as amended by Council Directive 63/21 (JO 1963 p. 62) and Council Directive 86/566 (OJ 1986 L332/22).
5. See List A of Annex I to the Directives.
6. Heading I of the Nomenclature of Capital Movements (Annex II to the Directives).
7. See, for example, *Royer, Jean Noël,* Case 48/75, [1976] ECR 497 at pp. 509–10.
8. For the purpose of this chapter, reference will be made to *Commission* v *Germany*, Case 205/84, 4 December 1986, [1987] 2 CMLR 69.
9. Art. 60
10. It raises, for example, the question whether a lawyer setting-up an office in another Member State can invoke the provisions of Council Directive 77/249 on the exercise by lawyers of freedom to provide services (OJ 1977 L78/17). See Usher, 'Establishment, Services and Lawyers' *Scots Law Times*, 23 February 1979, pp. 69–70.
11. OJ 1988 L172/1.

establishment takes, it is now clear from *Commission* v *France*,[12] that Member States may not treat companies differently for tax purposes, depending on the type of establishment present within their jurisdiction. It was there held that France could not treat the branches of foreign insurance companies, whose main offices were in other Member States, differently for the purpose of setting-off certain tax from those insurance companies which took the form of French-based companies which were subsidiaries of those foreign insurance companies. In the light of this it is intriguing to note that the proposed Second Banking Directive[13] distinguishes between branches and subsidiaries, treating the establishment of branches like the supply of services from another Member State, subject in principle to home state control. Furthermore, it was made clear that there was no way that restrictions could be imposed on the freedom of establishment in order to prevent tax evasion.[14] In so far as an undertaking formed in one Member State may wish to move its business activities to another Member State without re-registering as a company or firm formed under the law of the host state, a matter which previously had been thought by legal theorists to raise complex problems of the recognition of the artificial legal persons of another legal system,[15] the judgment of the Second Chamber in *Segers*[16] contains the statement that it is not relevant that a foreign company operates solely in another Member State, requiring such a company in effect to be granted equal treatment with companies of the host state despite its registered office being in another state. Admittedly, however, this case was concerned with rather technical matters of social security. The views of the legal theorists appear, however, to have been proved correct in

12. Case 270/83, 28 January 1986, [1987] 1 CMLR 401.
13. OJ 1988 C84/1.
14. The question of the extent to which tax considerations may limit freedom of establishment has been directly raised in the reference in *R* v *H.M. Treasury ex parte Daily Mail* [1987] 2 CMLR 1.
15. It had been held in Belguim, before UK Accession, that an English company moving its primary establishment to Belguim became wholly subject to Belgian company law ('Belgian Cour de Cassation', 12 November 1965, *Pasicrisle Belge*, 1966, p. 336), and it would appear that in French law a company would in principle be regarded as a nullity if its 'siège réel' was different from the country of incorporation (see, for example, Renauld, 'La reconnaissance mutuelle des sociétés dans le Marché Commun', *Revue pratique des sociétés civiles et commerciales*, 1968, p. 207 at p. 211).
16. *Segers (D.H.M.)* v *Bestuur Van de Bedrijfsvereniging Voor Bank en Verzekeringswezen, Groothandel en Vrije Beroepen*, Case 79/85, [1987] 2 CMLR 247, European Ct.

R v *HM Treasury ex parte Daily Mail*[17] where it was pointed out that companies exist only by virtue of national legislation and that the Treaty rules on freedom of establishment did not overcome the national law problems as to retention of legal personality on the transfer of the registered office or real head office to another Member State, so that they did not confer a right to transfer central management and control to another Member State. Hence a company incorporated under a system, such as the French, which requires the 'siège réel' to remain in the state of incorporation, will not be able to take advantage of primary establishment. It was suggested that in the case of companies, the right of establishment would usually be exercised by the setting-up of agencies, branches or subsidiaries.

On the other hand, in the light of what has happened in the financial services sector, it is perhaps worth observing that where establishment has been effected by natural persons, the European Court has been unwilling to enter into discussion as to whether a qualification obtained in one Member State is equivalent to the qualification required in the host Member State, unless there are rules of either national or European Community law providing for such recognition.[18]

SERVICES

Whilst the basic aim of the provisions on freedom of establishment may be to achieve equal treatment for those establishing themselves in a particular Member State with the nationals or companies of that Member State, equal treatment with nationals is not necessarily the main problem with regard to provision of services. This was realised in the earliest cases, such as *Van Binsbergen*,[19] or *Coenen*,[20] which in fact both involved the provision of services across a border by persons who were nationals of the country in which the service was to be provided, but resident in another Member State. If,

17. Case 81/87, 27 September 1988.
18. Compare *Ministère Public* v *Auer*, Case 136/78, [1979] ECR 437, where the court held that France could not be required to recognise an Italian veterinary qualification in the absence of any national or Community legislation to that effect, with *Auer* v *Ministère Public*, Case 271/82, [1983] ECR 2727, where it was held that France was obliged to recognise that qualification following the expiry of the time limit for implementing Council Directive 78/1026 (OJ 1978 L362/1) on the mutal recognition of qualifications in veterinary medicine.
19. *Johannes Henricus Maria van Binsbergen* v *Bestuur van de Bedrijfsvereniging voor de Metaalnijverheid*, Case 33/74, [1974] ECR 1299.
20. *Coenen, Robert Gerardus, and others* v *Sociaal-Economische Raad*, Case 39/75, [1975] ECR 1547.

however, the aim of freedom to provide services is the removal of obstacles to the provision of services rather than equal treatment with host state nationals, the question arises as to how far such freedom should go. If a comparison may be made with the much litigated area of the free movement of goods, it is widely thought that the case-law, particularly the famous *Cassis de Dijon*[21] case, has established the principle that goods sold in one Member State may be sold in another. However, whilst recognising the fundamental importance of this principle, the possibly heretical view could be put forward that in fact *Cassis de Dijon* represented a restriction of the earlier case-law, particularly with regard to national price legislation,[22] which had held such legislation to have an effect equivalent to a quantitative restriction even where it quite genuinely applied on the same basis to national and imported products, where it had the effect of making the sale of imported products more difficult than that of domestic products, if not impossible.

In this view, the real importance of the *Cassis de Dijon* decision is its recognition of the so-called mandatory requirements, that is requirements which Member States may in the absence of Community rules impose on goods imported from other Member States even though that may have the effect of restricting or even rendering impossible such importation. It may further be observed that high on this list of mandatory requirements comes the protection of consumers, a matter which was fundamental to the judgment of the European Court in the insurance cases.[23] Furthermore, the Treaty itself recognises as legitimate certain restrictions on the movement of goods laid down in art. 36, that is restrictions justified on grounds of public morality, public policy and public security, the protection of health and life of humans, animals or plants, the protection of national artistic, historic or archaeological treasures, and the protection of industrial and commercial property, provided, of course, that such restrictions do not constitute a means of arbitrary discrimination or a disguised restriction on trade between Member States. Nevertheless, it may still be asserted that it is only because of this case-law that the authors of the White Paper were able to assert that the single market could be completed by a specified number of directives.

It is therefore intriguing to observe that, despite the absence

21. *Rewe* v *Bundesmonopolverwaltung für Branntwein*, Case 120/78, [1979] ECR 649.
22. See, for example, *Tasca*, Case 65/75, [1976] ECR 291, at p. 308.
23. See *Commission* v *Germany*, Case 205/84, 4 December 1986, [1987] 2 CMLR 69, at paras 39 and 64.

of any equivalent of art. 36 in the field of the provision of services, the court has in fact invented permissible restrictions which parallel art. 36, and possibly also the so-called mandatory requirements. So, for example, the court has in *Debauve*[24] recognised that a Member State may enforce its public policy with regard to prohibition of advertising on television services provided from another Member State, and in *Coditel* v *Ciné Vog*,[25] the court recognised that intellectual property rights in a film could be protected again against a television showing of that film transmitted from another Member State.

On the other hand, the court has, since its decision in *Van Waesemael*,[26] recognised the concept of the equivalence of safeguards, holding that where a Member State requires certain safeguards to be complied with, the fact that the provider of the service complies with those same safeguards in his home state, is sufficient to allow a service to be provided. All this, it may be suggested, forms a necessary background to understanding the court's decisions in the insurance cases.

The policy issue which is raised is essentially whether the consumer in the context of the provision of services should have a choice between paying less and receiving fewer safeguards in return, and paying more and receiving greater protection, or whether Member States should be permitted to restrict this choice by insisting on certain minimum safeguards that must be met by every provider of the particular service. The response of the European Court seems to be that it depends on the economic level at which a particular activity is carried out, but it is worth again noting the special protection given to consumers, defined in the recent Consumer Credit Directive[27] as a natural person acting outside the scope of his trade or profession. To summarise *Commission* v *Germany*,[28] the court held that with regard to direct insurance effected through intermediaries, Germany was justified in requiring insurance undertakings established in other Member States to comply with its authorisation requirements in so far as they were necessary to ensure the protection of policy holders and insured persons.[29] This was irrespective of the fact that such insurance companies may be authorised in their home states, and provided that the insurance

24. *Procureur du Roi* v *Debauve, Marc, J.V.C. and others,* Case 52/79, [1980] ECR 833.
25. Case 67/79, [1980] ECR 881.
26. *Ministère Public* v *Van Waesemael*, Cases 110 and 111/78, [1979] ECR 35.
27. Council Directive 87/102 (OJ 1987 L42/48) art. 1(2)(a).
28. Case 205/84, 4 December 1986, [1987] 2 CMLR 69.
29. Ibid. para. 39.

companies were not required to duplicate conditions already met in their home state,[30] and given a situation in which Community law had harmonised solvency requirements but not the rules relating to 'technical reserves' or conditions of insurance.[31] It was, however, expressly recognised that there may be situations where, because of the nature of the risk insured and of the party seeking insurance, there was no need to protect the latter by the application of mandatory rules of his or her natural law.[32] In particular, the court held that, in the field of co-insurance, there was no justification for the German requirement that the leading insurer should be authorised by the German authorities. The arguments for consumer protection did not have the same force as in connection with other forms of insurance since, in the view of the court, co-insurance arises in the context of insurance taken out only by 'large undertakings or groups of undertakings which are in a position to assess and negotiate insurance policies proposed to them'. This distinction has been followed by the Second Insurance Directive,[33] which in effect provides freedom for large risks, but does not really provide freedom to provide insurance services across frontiers at the level of ordinary consumers. In any event, according to the court, Council Directive 78/473[34] already provided sufficient co-ordination and co-operation between supervisory authorities in the Member States. In neither case, however, did the court accept that a German requirement that the insurance undertakings should themselves be established in Germany had been shown to be indispensible;[35] indeed, it took the view that such a requirement would negate the freedom to provide services.[36]

It may be suggested that the basic 1973 Directive on the Freedom of Establishment and Freedom to Provide Services in relation to the activities of banks and other financial institutions,[37] in reality became redundant very shortly after it entered into force following the judgments of the European Court which held that the basic principles of freedom of establishment and freedom to provide services were in fact directly effective. If, however, a general comment could be made on the subsequent legislation which has

30. Ibid. para. 47.
31. Ibid. paras 37 to 40. See EC Council Directives 73/239 (OJ (1973) L228/3) and 79/267 (OJ 1979 L63/1).
32. Ibid. para. 49.
33. Directive 88/357, OJ 1988 L172/1.
34. OJ 1978, L151/25
35. *Commission* v *Germany*, Case 205/84, (see footnote 23), para. 56.
36. Ibid. para. 52.
37. OJ 1973 L194/1.

particularly concentrated on what are termed 'credit institutions', it may be suggested that the common feature of this legislation is to ensure certain common standards of supervision of credit institutions and to ensure that certain accounting principles are followed by banks and credit institutions; hence, the emphasis appears to be on control rather than freedom. The fundamental question is, of course, how far the one can exist without the other. On the other hand, the Unit Trusts Directive,[38] which would appear to have been regarded as the model for future development, is based on the concept that authorisation by the competent authorities of the home Member State is valid for all Member States[39] – essentially the principle urged by the Commission in the insurance cases. However, closer examination shows that Member States may apply their own marketing and advertising rules to UCITS situated in another Member State.[40] The use of home state control is the policy envisaged in the White Paper, but it is interesting to note that the proposed Second Banking Directive[41] distinguishes between home control of branches (and of the supply of services) and host state control of the establishment of subsidiaries, although of course the latter are by definition created under local law. In effect it treats setting up a branch as if it were provision of services from another Member State, rather than a form of establishment. It would be foolish to imagine that Community rules easing the exercise of freedom of establishment and freedom to provide services will necessarily be deregulatory in nature. The implementation of the Second Directive is dependent upon the simultaneous entry into force of Community legislation on 'own funds' and solvency ratios, according to its recitals. A proposal for a directive on the latter was published in April 1988.[42]

It may finally be noted in the context of the Treaty rules on the provision of services that one specific measure which has not been altered by the Single European Act is art. 61(2) which states that the liberalisation of banking and insurance services connected with movements of capital shall be effected in step with the progressive liberalisation of the movement of capital. Hence a clear express link is drawn between the Treaty rules on provision of services and those rules relating to the movement of money, a matter

38. EC Council Directive 85/611 on 'Undertakings for collective investment in transferable securities (UCITS)' (OJ (1985) L375/3).
39. Art. 4(1).
40. Arts 44 and 45.
41. OJ 1988 C84/1.
42. OJ 1988 C135/4.

noted in the recitals to the proposed Second Banking Directive, and applied in a restrictive way by the European Court in *P. Van Eycke* v *ASPA S.A.*[43] Here it was held that since the opening of a savings account in another Member State was not yet liberated under the capital movements directives, it was not a breach of the Treaty provisions on freedom to provide services for Belgium to limit tax exemptions on such accounts to deposits in local currency at credit institutions having their head office (*siège social*) in Belgium. Presumably such rules will have to be changed when a Community law right to set up savings accounts in other Member States comes into operation.

COMPETITION

It has been clear since the decision in the *Züchner* case[44] that in terms of Community competition law, banks are not special, in other words they are not in themselves regarded as being entrusted with the operation of services of general economic interest. Hence, in that case it was made clear that if there was a concerted practice with regard to the charges made for the transfer of funds from one Member State to another, then that would be a breach of art. 85(1). It also appears from the German fire insurance cases[45] that even where the market is tightly controlled, as was the case in the German insurance market before the judgment in *Commission* v *Germany*,[46] the competition rules apply at least in so far as there is scope left for competition, repeating a view which had already been taken with regard to certain agricultural sectors, for example. The judgment in these cases also reveals the intriguing thought that even if an agreement appears to relate only to the national market, nevertheless if it affects the branches in that market of companies based in other Member States it may be capable of affecting trade between Member States within the meaning of art. 85(1).

Since the court's decision in *Züchner* the Commission has issued a number of formal decisions in the banking sector which give some indication of the types of restriction which it is prepared to tolerate. Hence, it accepted that exemption could be given to

43. Case 267/86, 21 September 1988.
44. *Züchner* v *Bayerische Vereinsbank*, Case 172/80, [1981] ECR 2021.
45. *Verband der Sachversicherer eV (supported by Gesamtverband der deutschen Versicherungswirtschaft eV, Intervener)* v *EC Commission*, Case 45/85, 27 January 1987, *The Times*, 7 February 1987.
46. Case 205/84, 4 December 1986, [1987] 2 CMLR 69.

the Eurocheque system[47] in so far as it led to improvements of the payment system and benefit to users, the uniform conditions being indispensable in the view of the Commission where the system involved a non-reciprocal service by the payee banks. It was further accepted that the uniform fixing of a maximum guaranteed amount, for example, was indispensable for the operation of such system. On the other hand, it was made clear that agreements at the national level fixing commissions were not indispensable, and had the effect of eliminating residual competition. In the case of the Irish banks,[48] a negative clearance was given with regard to their agreements concerning opening hours (which at first sight hardly seems beneficial for consumers), clearing rules, and their direct debiting scheme, although the Commission expressly reserved its position with regard to interest rates, as it also did, in rather greater detail, in the Italian banks case.[49] There, express exemption was also given with regard to agreements on the collection and/or acceptance of Italian bills and documents, on the collection of bank cheques and similar instruments payable in Italy, and on a new uniform type of lira traveller's cheque.

The interesting point, however, with regard to the application of the competition rules in the financial services sector must surely be the question of agreements relating to interest rates.[50] Before the judgment in *Züchner*, the Commission had suggested, in answer to a written question in the European Parliament, that inter-bank agreements on interest rates could be considered as monetary policy instruments of the Member States.[51] However, following the *Züchner* judgment, Commissioner Andriessen suggested[52] that interest rates should not be governed by inter-bank agreements even if they were approved, authorised or promoted by the competent national authorities. More recently, Commissioner Sutherland is reported as having stated that, 'the osmosis which sometimes exists between supervisory authorities and those they supervise blurs a distinction between genuine monetary policy and cartels'.[53] It may be observed that the decisions relating respectively to Irish and Italian banks expressly refrain from deciding whether interest rate agreements breach the competition rules or not. One aspect of the matter came

47. Commission Decision 85/77 (OJ 1985 L35/43).
48. Commission Decision 86/507 (OJ 1986 L295/28).
49. Commission Decision 87/103 (OJ 1987 L43/51).
50. See Dassesse and Isaacs, *EEC Banking Law*, 1985, pp. 37–9.
51. WQ 199/79 (OJ 1979 C213/6).
52. Speech cited in Dassesse and Isaacs, footnote 50, p. 38.
53. Agence Europe No. 4543, 6 May 1987, at p. 9.

before the European Court in *P. Van Eycke* v *ASPA S.A.*[54], where the view appears to have been taken that it was in order for national legislation itself to lay down the maximum rates of interest to be paid on deposit accounts in order to benefit from tax exemption. It would, however, be a breach of the Treaty rules for the legislation to require or incite deposit-holders to follow the terms of a previous agreement between credit institutions (which in practice had not been universally followed). This gives rise to a very subtle distinction: it is permissible for national legislation itself to lay down rules as to interest rates, but it is not permissible for national legislation to order banks to follow an agreement reached between the banks themselves.

Again, however, the policy question remains: should competition with regard to interest rates be permitted even to the extent that it might affect exchange rates? Or, on the other hand, should exchange rates and interest rates be the fixed parameters within which competition may take place?

CAPITAL AND CURRENT PAYMENTS

The free movement of capital is the only one of the basic freedoms established by the EEC Treaty which has not been held to be directly effective by the European Court. In its judgment in the leading case of *Casati*,[55] the court explained this partly on the relationship between the movement of capital and monetary and economic policy in general. Given that art.67(1) of the Treaty only requires the free movement of capital in so far as that is necessary for the achievement of the Common Market, the court took the view that the assessment of what was necessary was a matter for the Council, and on looking at the relevant Council directives,[56] it noted that there was no obligation on Member States to liberalise the movement of bank notes. The case arose from a breach of Italian exchange control legislation which involved the re-export of German bank notes from Italy after their holder had failed to achieve his intention of using them to buy a piece of machinery in Italy. Having found that there was no obligation to liberalise the movement of bank notes, the court then took the view that there was no need for

54. Case 267/86, 21 September 1988.
55. *Casati Guerrino*, Case 203/80, [1981] ECR 2595.
56. Council Directive of 11 May 1960 (JO 1960 p. 921), as amended by Council Directive 63/21 (JO 1963 p. 62) and Council Directive 86/566 (OJ 1986 L332/22).

a Member State to use the procedures laid down by art. 73 of the Treaty in order to restrict the movement of bank notes.

Turning to art. 106 of the Treaty which requires Member States to authorise payments in the currency of the Member State in which the creditor resides in relation to services of goods provided by virtue of the provisions of the Treaty relating to the free movement of goods, or freedom to provide services, the court took the view that this provision did not require Member States to allow the movement of bank notes if such movement was not necessary and indeed standard practice in relation to the transaction in question. By way of parenthesis, one might perhaps wonder whether the court's view of standard practice in relation to the habits of small businessmen was in fact wholly accurate. Hence, again, the court found that the powers of a Member State were not limited at all where there was no obligation to liberalise the movement of bank notes. Furthermore, the court found that the transaction in question could not be an invisible transaction within the meaning of art. 106(3), where the money was in fact being re-exported from the state in which it was supposed to have been spent. The view expressed in *Casati* that there is no requirement to allow cash payments was followed in *Lambert,*[57] where the court upheld Luxembourg (and Belgian) rules requiring payments for exports to be by credit transfer or by cheque, to be converted on the regulated market rather than the free market.

It was, however, firmly established by the court that art. 106(1) concerning current payments could have direct effect in so far as the transaction to which it related was already liberalised under the Treaty in *Luisi and Carbone*.[58] This case, which involved amongst other things medical expenses and touring expenses, is particularly noticeable for the fact that the court defined the Treaty provisions on services as including the freedom for the recipient of a service to go to another Member State to receive that service there, an interpretation which, it may be suggested, means that virtually any movement of persons between Member States is capable of falling within the scope of the Treaty. The court held that the third paragraph of art. 106 on invisible transactions was in fact subordinate to the first paragraph on current payments, and then set about defining the concept of current payments as opposed to capital. It took the view in principle that current payments

57. *Ministère Public* v *Lambert, René,* Case 308/86, 14 July 1988, (OJ 1988 C215/11).

58. *Luisi, Graziana and Carbone, Giuseppe* v *Ministero del Tesoro*, Cases 262/82 and 26/83, [1984] ECR 377.

constitute the consideration within the context of an underlying transaction, whereas movements of capital are essentially concerned with the investment of funds. In particular, the court held that the transfer of bank notes does not constitute a movement of capital where it corresponds to an obligation to pay for goods or services. It was however accepted that art. 106 only applies to liberalise current payments made in the currency of the state of the creditor, although notice may be taken of the early decision of the English Court of Appeal in *Schorsch Meier*[59] that art. 106 empowered a national court actually to give judgment in that currency, an interpretation which appears to go rather further than that given by the European Court itself. The court did also accept that Member States were entitled to control the genuineness of current payments and to use flat rate limits as a prima facie test for determining what was a current payment. However, the European Court has more recently applied a restrictive literal approach to art. 106 in *Lambert*,[60] holding that it is not relevant to the way an exporter receives payment, merely being concerned to ensure that the importer is able to make the payment. It may respectfully be suggested that both aspects are equally important to the achievement of the genuine free movement of goods and services, and that this judgment takes an unduly narrow approach.

Although the court, therefore, endeavoured to make a clear distinction between movements of capital and current payments, it remains the case that the series of directives on the free movement of capital enacted under art. 67 of the Treaty appear to cover both types of transaction.[61] Although, intriguingly, they require transfers in respect of capital movements to be made on the same exchange rate conditions as those governing payments relating to current transactions, a terminology which appears to recognise that there are two different concepts. In the version resulting from Directive 86/566,[62] which in effect merged the old lists A and B and added certain other elements to those lists, list A, which is a list of transactions which must be liberalised, includes direct investments, as has already been mentioned, but excludes purely financial investments giving an indirect means of moving into the capital market. The list does however expressly include transfers in

59. *Schorsch Meier GmbH* v *Hennin* [1975] QB 416.
60. Case 308/86, 14 July 1988.
61. Council Directive of 11 May 1960 (JO 1960 p. 921), as amended by Council Directive 63/21 (JO 1963 p. 62) and Council Directive 86/566 (OJ 1986 L332/22).
62. OJ 1986 L332/22.

performance of insurance contracts 'as and when free movement in respect of services' is extended to them. It may be suggested that this adds little to the effect of the first paragraph of art. 106 on current payments, and makes the distinction drawn in the insurance cases between the types of insurance services which may be offered by companies established in another Member State and those which may not, without a further authorisation, of even greater importance. Indeed, list A does actually expressly include transfers of monies required for the provision of services, which is a clear overlap with the concept of current payments enounced in *Luisi and Carbone*.

On the other hand, list C which defines the transactions whose liberalisation is not required, includes the opening and the placing of funds on current or deposit accounts, and the physical import and export of financial assets. The fact that such movements may still be restricted is of course of theoretical interest given the current situation in the UK, but remains of considerable interest for a number of other Member States. Complete liberalisation from 1 July 1990 is envisaged in Directive 88/361,[63] but not without strings. Proposals aimed at eliminating or reducing risks of tax evasion and tax avoidance are required to be put forward and considered during the interim period.

However, even where liberalisation is expressly required by Community legislation, derogations from that liberalisation have been permitted and will continue to be possible under the 1988 Directive, albeit by a somewhat more restricted procedure (though it may be doubted whether the terms of a directive may prevent the exercise of powers which will still exist under the Treaty itself). In this context, it may be observed that the procedure laid down in the section of the Treaty concerned with capital movements in art. 73 to authorise restrictions, has not in practice been used. Rather, restrictions have been authorised under art. 108 which is concerned with the balance of payments or, more accurately, the protection of the balance of payments of a Member State. In its judgment in *Brugnoni and Ruffinengo*,[64] the court seemed to accept that art. 5 of the Capital Movement Directive[65] allows controls indispensable to prevent breaches of safeguard measures authorised

63. OJ 1988 L178/7.
64. *Brugnoni, Luigi and Ruffinengo, Roberto* v *Cassa di risparmio di Genova & Imperia*, Case 157/85, [1986] ECR 2013.
65. Council Directive of 11 May 1960 (JO 1960 p. 921), as amended by Council Directive 63/21 (JO 1963 p. 62) and Council Directive 86/566 (OJ 1986 L332/22).

under art. 108. However, it also accepted that a decision taken in 1985 under art. 108 could continue safeguards originally enacted in 1974 to protect the balance of payments. One may wonder whether there really could be said to have been a threat to the Italian balance of payments continuing throughout all that time, and it is of some interest to note that following the extension of the liberalised capital movements by Directive 86/566,[66] additional safeguard measures were enacted in favour of those Member States which were at that stage permitted to restrict otherwise liberalised movements,[67] to allow protective measures under art. 108(3) with regard to operations newly liberalised under the directive.

To make a further comparison with the free movement of goods, the point may be taken that when the Commission gives a Member State authorisation under art. 115 not to grant Community treatment to goods in free circulation in another Member State, having been imported from a third country, the court has consistently held that since this is a derogation from one of the fundamental freedoms of the Treaty, the Commission must take great care when exercising its powers. In particular, it appears both from the *Kaufhof* case[68] and the *Ilford* case[69] that the Commission must be satisfied both that the Member State is authorised as a matter of Community law to have the measure of commercial policy whose protection it is seeking, and that the threatened importations would actually be likely to endanger that policy. Unfortunately, in *Brugnoni and Ruffinengo*, there appears to be no real discussion as to whether the Commission is under a duty when using art. 108 to investigate the seriousness of any threat to the balance of payments of the Member State, and whether the transactions in question would be likely to threaten the balance of payments. The specific provision in art. 3 of the 1988 Directive, however, requires the Commission to consult the Monetary Committee and the Committee of Governors of the Central Banks, and is subject to a power of revocation or amendment in the Council.

Be that as it may, in so far as the directives do operate without derogation, they will not include what ordinary private citizens would regard as the free movement of money, that is the ability freely to move cash or to open current accounts, until mid 1990.

66. OJ 1986 L332/22.
67. Commission Decisions 87/150 (Ireland), 87/151 (Italy) and 87/152 (Greece) (OJ 1987 L63/34, 36 and 38).
68. *Kaufhof AG* v *Commission of the European Communities*, Case 29/75, [1976] ECR 431.
69. *Ilford SpA* v *Commission of the European Communities*, Case 1/84R, [1984] ECR 423, [1984] 2 CMLR 475.

The policy question remains, however, as to whether it is desirable that such a freedom should be established before the European Monetary System[70] and the European Currency Unit[71] are uniformly applied and recognised, or indeed whether one should wait until a further stage of monetary integration. The published view of the Economic and Social Committee, which brings together both sides of industry, is that liberalisation cannot be achieved without stabilisation of exchange rates.[72]

Whilst it is beyond the scope of this chapter to describe in detail the workings of the European Monetary System, the basis of its exchange rate mechanism is that each participating currency has a 'central rate' fixed against the European Currency Unit (ECU), subject to a fluctuation margin of + 2.25% (or + 6% in the case of Italy), and that a 'threshold of divergence', which may trigger corrective measures, is fixed at 75% of the maximum spread of divergence set for each currency; adjustments of central rates require mutual agreement of the participating Member States. Whilst it is not, therefore, a rigid system of fixed exchange rates, it offers a degree of relative stability in a world of floating exchange rates. An element of responsiveness in the system arises from the fact that the central rate is fixed against the ECU, which is a 'basket' currency unit defined in terms of the sum of fixed elements of the national currencies which make up the basket (that is, 0.0878 pound sterling, 1.13 French francs, 0.719 German marks, etc.). The overall value of the basket depends on the daily value of these currency elements, but these fixed elements do not change automatically when central rates are altered or market values fluctuate, so that the percentage composition of the unit in terms of national currencies may change: the percentage share of a currency which rises in value will increase, and that of a currency whose value diminishes will decrease. The 1978 Resolution of the European Council expressly provides[73] that any revision of the relative weights of the currencies must not modify the overall external value of the ECU, which was originally required to be the same as that of the previous European Unit of Account (EUA) created in 1975, which in turn was based on the value in June 1974 of the 'Special Drawing Rights' of the International Monetary

70. Created by the Resolution of the European Council of 5 December 1987 (EC Bulletin 1978 No. 12 point 1.1.11) and EC Council Regulation 3181/78 (OJ 1978 L379/2).

71. Defined by Council Regulation 3180/78 (OJ 1978 L379/1) as amended by Council Regulation 2626/84 (OJ 1984 L247/1).

72. OJ 1988 C175/1.

73. Art. 2(3).

Fund (SDR).[74] This was also a 'basket' unit, but giving a heavy weighting to the United States dollar, which is not included in the ECU basket. The original value of the SDR was based on the gold value of the US dollar,[75] which also happened to be the value of the old unit of account originally used by the European Communities.[76] Despite the historical interest of this element of continuity in Community units of account, it may perhaps be suggested that it is the absence of any reference to the dollar in the current ECU which has led to its growing use as a denominator of long-term loans in the financial markets.

Indeed, it must be emphasised that in the modern world the Community can hardly be treated in isolation in matters of monetary policy. Therefore, it may be suggested that one of the more positive provisions in the Single European Act is the amendment to art.70(1) of the EEC Treaty, which enables the Council to enact legislation concerning the movement of capital to non-Member States by a qualified majority, except in so far as such measures may constitute a step backwards from the existing level of liberalisation, in which case unanimity would be required. One might therefore wonder if we are about to witness the beginning of a common monetary policy of the Community towards the outside world – or would that be too much to hope for? One of the first results of the revised art. 70(1) is art. 7 of the 1988 capital movements directive, under which Member States shall endeavour to attain the same degree of liberalisation in their treatment of transfers in respect of movements of capital to or from third countries as that which applies to operations with residents of Member States. On the other hand, art. 7 of the proposed Second Banking Directive has acquired a certain notoriety for its insistence on reciprocity in the context of the acquisition of participations in credit undertakings and the establishment of European Community subsidiaries by third country undertakings.

74. Council Decision of 21 April 1975.

75. International Monetary Fund Articles of Agreement art. xxi section 2; see Mann, *Legal Aspects of Money*, 4th ed., 1982, pp. 507–8.

76. See Usher, 'Financing the Community' in *Thirty Years of Community Law*, 1983, pp. 195–6.

2—1992 - ITS IMPACT ON EUROPEAN BANKS, THEIR STRUCTURE, OPERATIONS AND ACCOUNTS

Michael Fowle

INTRODUCTION

Commentaries on the impact of 1992 on the financial services industry usually refer to an institution known as a 'bank'. Each member states' supervisors have their own definition of a bank, while the European Commission prefers the term 'credit institution'. It might be useful to consider what in commercial terms we are discussing.

'Credit institution' is a wide-ranging term and encompasses a variety of businesses throughout Europe. It embraces not only the 'universal banks' of West Germany, the UK and France, but also the UK discount houses and building societies, merchant and investment banks, savings banks, mortgage banks, farmers' and craftsmens' banks, postal banks, and a whole range of different types of co-operatives. The definition provided in the First Banking Directive[1] is:

> . . . an undertaking whose business is to receive deposits or other repayable funds from the public and to grant credit for its own account.

But the draft Second Directive[2] annexes a list of activities which banks may be authorised to conduct. This range implies a model of a 'universal bank' and has been taken to suggest that the Commission is primarily interested in developing the opportunities for the universal bank. However, the new regime will apply equally to all institutions and will give them all the same basic rights.

This chapter primarily addresses the effect of 1992 on the institutions best placed to adopt Europe as their domestic market.

1. First Banking Directive: 77/780
2. Proposed Second Banking Directive: COM (87) 715 (final)

Thus, inevitably, it concentrates on the universal banks since they have the greatest resources and the most developed networks in Europe.

THE EUROPEAN MARKET

The European banking sector operates in an environment which is still largely determined by the 12 individual Member States. The First Banking Directive (adopted by the Council of the European Community in 1977) established some basic principles, principally in respect of minimum supervisory requirements, but did little to remove the barriers to integration.

The historical effects of protective measures, combined with cultural and economic differences, are evident in the variety of market structures in the community. For instance, the Spanish and Italian markets support a large number of smaller institutions, mostly regional in nature, which have been protected from competitive influences by the conservatism of their administrators and by a pervasive regionalism. In these markets, as with the French market, the restrictions over access to stock exchanges have prevented the emergence of the truly 'universal' bank. Widespread state ownership of banking institutions in France and Italy has tended to encourage a static and uncompetitive market in which banks have become bureaucratic instruments of government policy rather than purely commercial enterprises.

Meanwhile, the more liberal approach of the UK, West Germany and the Netherlands has allowed banks to develop in a more open market. With the impetus provided by deregulation in the investment business and the lifting of exchange controls, these countries have developed institutions which are more universal in the range of services which they can offer. The relative accessibility of these markets has resulted in greater competition and more innovatory product development, in both the wholesale and retail sectors. In this environment, larger institutions have emerged and won substantial market share in their home markets, since only they can support the costs of wide ranging product development.

The outcome for the European market is that wholesale activities, being involved in the transmission of funds in unrestricted currencies, have gravitated to the least regulated and most efficient and honest market – London. This has given London a dominant share of the global market. However, European retail markets are extremely fragmented, so that even National Westminster Bank and Deutsche Bank, two of Europe's major banks, between them only account for 6% of the total European market.

The principal features of regulation in the major European markets are too numerous for inclusion in this chapter, but apart from significant restrictions on foreign banks imposed by the southern European countries, the principal features of the present regulatory arrangements are:

(a) The branch endowment capital requirement which is operated by all countries except the UK. This is a major operational constraint in that it reduces banks' control over the allocation of their resources. It thereby deprives them of the flexibility which is required to meet varying market conditions.
(b) The differences between the member states' regulations and procedures, which increase the administrative burden of compliance and complicate the process of expansion into new markets. However, such differences are generally regarded as irritating rather than seriously restrictive. Variations in the definition of endowment capital have been cited as such an irritant.

There are also numerous cultural and commercial differences which distort the trans-European market, but it is difficult and inappropriate to enumerate them in this chapter. *Research on the Cost of Non-Europe*[3] (vol. 9 p. 62), published by the Commission, identified the following areas of regulation through which member states disrupt the European market:

(a) Barriers to establishment in banking:

  (i) restrictions on the legal form banks may adopt;
  (ii) limitations on the number of branches that may be established;
  (iii) restrictions on the takeover of domestic banks;
  (iv) restrictions of equity or other control of domestic banks.

(b) Barriers to operating conditions in banking:

  (i) the need to maintain separate capital funds;
  (ii) differences in the definition of 'own capital' funds;
  (iii) the need to maintain certain capital-asset ratios;
  (iv) exchange controls.

3. 'Research on the Cost of Non-Europe', published by the Commission of the European Communities, Luxembourg, 1988.

(c) Barriers to competing for business in banking:

(i) limitations on services offered;
(ii) restrictions on local retail banking;
(iii) restrictions on acquisition of securities and other assets.

The securities industry has become increasingly significant to banks, as commercial banks seek a wider range of financing and the retail sector becomes more aware of the attractions of the stock markets. The industry is even more protected than the pure banking sector. As well as the restrictions imposed by banking supervisors on the banks' ability to enter the business, there are major barriers specific to the securities industry:

(a) Barriers to establishment in securities:

(i) membership of some stock exchanges is limited to national citizens;
(ii) constraints on the establishment of offices to solicit and carry out business in secondary markets;
(iii) restrictions on the takeover of or equity participation in domestic institutions;
(iv) limitations on the establishment of securities firms in a universal banking system.

(b) Barriers to operating conditions in securities:

(i) exchange controls and other equivalent measures which prevent or limit the purchase of foreign securities;
(ii) conflicting national prudential requirements for investor protection;
(iii) discriminatory taxes on the purchase of foreign securities.

(c) Barriers to competing for business in securities:

(i) limited access to primary markets in terms of lead management of domestic issues;
(ii) restricted access to secondary markets because of national stockbroker monopolies on some stock exchanges;
(iii) restrictions on dealing with investing public.

The features described above are the principle cause of the price differentials identified in *Research on the Cost of Non-Europe* (Vol. 9, pp. 30 and 31), where assumed potential price reductions in the overall financial services sector range from 21% in Spain to 4%

in the Netherlands. Within this range, the European market falls into three broad categories:

(a) *Low impact* countries (UK, West Germany, Netherlands and Denmark) where competition is strongest and profitability is at reasonable levels because of the advanced state of the market: 1992 is unlikely to affect the home market significantly.
(b) *Middle impact* countries (France, Belgium, Italy and Ireland) where prices are low but costs tend to be higher: competition is inhibited in some respects and 1992 will therefore have some impact on home markets since prices will be open to challenge from more efficient institutions.
(c) *High impact* countries (Spain, Portugal and Greece) where prices are highest but the protective environment creates cost inefficiencies: the impact on home markets will be significant as lower cost competitors will be able to undercut domestic institutions.

Financial institutions in several countries dispute the detail of the results given in vol. 9 of the *Research on the Cost of Non-Europe*, but few deny that regulation causes cost differentials.

CHANGES CURRENTLY IN PROGRESS

The process of transforming this fragmented market and loosening the constraints imposed by regulation relies on many factors. Before discussing the regulatory aspects, it should be remembered that important changes are taking place in the thinking both of the banking fraternity and of the customers which they serve. Not long ago the 'Common Market' was generally regarded as a bureaucratic imposition rather than a reality, but Lord Cockfield's ambitious initiative transformed the situation by reviving the European vision. The banking sector is itself influenced by this process – and, more importantly, the banking sector is confronted by potentially profound changes in its customer base. It is this cultural seachange which makes the legislative programme so important to the banking community.

The European Commission has initiated a series of directives:

(a) The Directive on the Abolition of Restrictions on The Movement of Capital, adopted by the Council in June 1988.[4]

4. Movement of Capital Directive: 88/361

(b) The draft Second Banking Directive, adopted by the Commission in January 1988; presently under discussion in the European Parliament.
(c) The Bank Accounts Directive, adopted by the Council in late 1986, but not yet implemented at national level.[5]
(d) The draft Investment Business Directive, which has been adopted by the Commission and is under consideration by the Council and Parliament.[6]
(e) The draft Mortgage Credit Directive[7]; proposed in 1985 but still not adopted.
(f) The draft Branch Accounts Directive;[8] agreed already in principle and likely to be adopted very soon by the Council.
(g) The Consolidated Supervision Directive of 1983.[9]
(h) The draft Own Funds Directive, adopted by the Commission in September 1986, with amended proposals published January 1988.[10]
(i) The draft Directive on Reorganisation and Winding-up, adopted by the Commission in December 1985, with amendments proposed in January 1988.[11]
(j) The draft Solvency Ratio Directive, submitted to the Council in April 1988.[12]

Between them, it is envisaged that these directives will create the basic conditions to enable banks to operate in a more truly European market. Of these, perhaps the directives concerning movement of capital, banking and investment services regulation and the linked topic of capital adequacy have the greatest impact and merit a brief explanation.

Freedom of movement of capital

This directive will result in the elimination of all remaining exchange controls within the European Community by the early 1990s: although Member States will have some freedom to restrict financial flows in cases of extreme difficulty, this legislation is fundamental to the entire 1992 programme. Given the central role of the banking

5. Bank Accounts Directive: 86/635(5)
6. Proposed investment services in the securities field COM (88) 778 — Syn 176
7. Proposed Mortgage Credit Directive: 84/730
8. Proposed Branch Accounts Directive: COM (88) 118 (final)
9. Consolidated Supervision Directive: 83/350
10. Own Funds Directive: COM (88) 15 (final)
11. Winding-up Directive: 85/788 (proposal)
12. Proposed Solvency Ratio Directive: COM (88) 194 (final)

market in allocating capital resources this can be regarded as the single most important step in the harmonisation of the market for financial services: without it, there would be little reason to proceed with the banking directives.

Of equal significance is the speed with which the legislation was approved by the Council, revealing the substantial political backing that '1992' has developed.

The Second Banking Directive and Investment Services Directive

In its draft of the Second Banking Directive the Commission has amended its approach considerably from that of the 1960s and 1970s, when its objective was to create truly harmonised regulatory and market conditions – an extremely difficult task. Instead, it has opted for the concept of mutual recognition – in other words, subject to the fulfillment of certain basic requirements, all national regulatory authorities will be regarded as operating acceptable supervisory regimes.

This concept creates the conditions in which the operation of an institution can be authorised and largely regulated by the institution's home authorities – once it meets its own authorities' requirements there is no reason why other Member States should need to repeat the process.

As mentioned above, another important feature of the draft Second Banking Directive is the definition of the business which it seeks to regulate. The simple definition of a credit institution in the First Banking Directive is no longer regarded as sufficient. Rather than attempting to redefine banking in terms which adequately describe the current nature of the business, the Commission has provided a list of activities which credit institutions may be authorised to conduct. Once the home regulator is satisfied that a credit institution is competent to transact a category of business included on the list and has granted authorisation for that business, the institution will be able to conduct it throughout the EC.

It should be noted that the list represents the widest permitted range of activities. Credit institutions will still be subject to any restrictions imposed under the legislation operated by their home regulator. Thus, banks in the UK and Germany will enjoy the widest range of opportunities, while it appears that banks based in Italy or Denmark will be subject to considerable restriction. The UK and German based banks will be free to provide all authorised products to Italy and Denmark while banks based in those countries may not be able to offer the same range either at home or abroad. Particular classes of business may still be subject to tighter controls – thus UK building societies, for example, will be regulated separately from banks. A degree of competitive relaxation in regulatory issues might be a consequence as regulators attempt to retain or attract business by creating a less onerous regime.

To some extent, the directive is retricted in scope. Its provisions are aimed at achieving:

(a) the freedom to engage in cross-border banking;
(b) the freedom to establish branches;
(c) the abolition of branch capital requirements;
(d) freedom from restrictions imposed by host EC countries on the range of permitted activities.

However, the directive only sets out to harmonise the process of initial authorisation and the supervision of financial soundness in relation to credit risk. Harmonisation does not extend to the regulation of conduct of business or to the aspects of financial soundness affected by, for example, position risk. Local regulators will continue to have some responsibility in these areas.

Thus, unless further harmonisation is imposed, the UK, for example, will presumably continue to apply the Consumer Credit Act and the Financial Services Act to all relevant business conducted in the UK, from whatever source. As the British Bankers Association has observed ('Commentary to the Directive', March 1988), it is unclear whether the prohibition on variable rate mortgages, which applies in Germany, will apply to banks offering the product from other Member States. Similar instances can be found elsewhere.

The directive specifically gives host countries a responsibility for supervising capital adequacy in relation to position risk. Many institutions will doubtless urge the Council to depart from this approach in the finalised directive, but if the article remains it will create a complex and burdensome environment.

The draft Investment Services Directive, which is at a far less advanced stage, extends similar principles of mutual recognition to non-bank investment businesses. In promulgating this draft, the Commission has indicated that the principles should include the mutual recognition of risk-based capital adequacy requirements.

It is recognised that both the Investment Services and Second Bank Co-ordination Directives must progress towards simultaneous implementation in order to ensure that *all* participants in the financial sector enjoy the same rights throughout the European market.

The concept of reciprocity introduced in the Second Banking Directive has received wide attention. The basic principle is that any non-EC bank wishing to establish within the EC will be automatically referred to the European Commission which will check that EC-Member States enjoy the same rights of establishment within the non-EC country. If the Commission finds that the banks of EC-Member States are not allowed to establish in the third country, then the proposal is that such banks will be barred from establishment. This provision has been widely criticised, particularly in the UK, because on some interpretations it might damage London as the hub of the global financial markets and because it represents a significant increase in the role of the Commission in banking regulation. Rather than a 'reserve power', the power proposed is one of automatic referral of new banks. As a minimum, critics wish to restrict the power so that it is invoked only on the behest of a particular Member State. Others suggest that as virtually all of the world's greatest banks already operate in the Community, the clause is of little significance.

Consolidated supervision, own funds, solvency ratios and securities-related requirements

Directives have only been drafted so far in respect of banking operations. Between them, these directives will create the mechanism for harmonised supervision of banks' financial condition by the following means:

(a) supervisors are required to assess banking groups on a consolidated basis as well as individually;
(b) components of institutions' 'own capital' will be standardised;
(c) standard risk weightings for both on balance sheet and off-balance sheet items.

In view of the work being conducted by the Bank for International Settlement (BIS) on the subject of capital adequacy it is likely that the final directives will converge with the BIS proposals. The capital adequacy directives will only define the minimum requirements: each national supervisor will be able to devise more restricted definitions of own capital and more prudent weightings, reflecting their assessment of risk in the home market for which they are responsible.

The draft directive on capital requirements for the securities business is due to be published in 1989. It will probably be based on risk assessments to some extent. Although such an approach has been adopted in the UK under the Financial Services Act 1986, it is not common in the other European markets where banks dominate the securities industry. Some difficulty may therefore be expected in devising a method which satisfies the cultural diversity of the European securities industry: doubtless a compromise will be reached between the risk-based approach and the 'global' basis preferred in Europe.

Taken together, the directives will remove the principal regulatory barriers and thereby enable banks to meet the demands of the newly-integrated European market.

BANKS' OPERATIONS

The Community's programme is unique, but the changes in Europe share some characteristics with the concurrent relaxation of the prohibition of inter-state banking in the United States. In fact, Europe has probably actually suffered less than the United States from cross-border restrictions over branch banking but even so there are striking similarities in that both environments have:

(a) tended to restrict retail markets rather than wholesale;
(b) forced banks to concentrate their resources in their home state; and
(c) created markets which are smaller than the service capacity afforded by modern technology.

In the states of the United States which have rescinded the ban on inter-state branch banking the regional banks have been quick to respond by expanding their operations and rationalising the methods of service delivery. Expansion has generaly been achieved by agreed takeover or merger, for the following reasons:

(a) banks must retain proximity to the retail markets which they service: cross-border marketing is not entirely suitable for retail customers;
(b) setting up branch networks from scratch is an expensive and high-risk approach;
(c) locally entrenched banks have usually obtained the best locations for their branch networks.

The expansions have permitted the new institutions to respond to local market conditions by retaining the staff of the acquired banks and by maintaining original corporate identities, at least for the purpose of client service. Investment in more centralised payment transmission systems has achieved savings in the cost of transaction processing, since fewer centres are required to handle the business of the same number of branches. Product development and advertising have tended to become more centralised, which has improved the cost-effectiveness of the selling process, and similar changes in administrative structure have led to a reduction in operational overheads. Most importantly, payment clearing facilities have been improved by investing in larger central systems, which provide a cheaper and more efficient service to the new, geographically dispersed, customer base.

Among the banks that have embarked on this process, First Union Corporation of North Carolina has achieved growth rates which, if sustained into the 1990s, would result in net assets at the current level of Citicorp.

The inter-state banking expansion has highlighted the increasing importance of:

(a) *Sound and coherent business strategy*: The dangers of expansion simply for its own sake are now generally well known, thanks to the effects of the uncoordinated and ill-conceived acquisition programmes of the 1970s. This lesson is being put into use in the current restructuring.
(b) *Cost control*: In the absence of business strategy, cost control becomes more difficult, and unless appropriate procedures are quickly imposed upon enlarged groups, unproductive expenditure can escalate. The new expanding groups are much more disciplined in this respect and this is a key element in improving return on capital.
(c) *Rigorous control over the loan book and loan provisioning*: Banks have suffered from the urge to lend simply in order to achieve market share and sheer size: risk assessment and monitoring were not given sufficient attention. The cost of inadequate control is evident and, again, the successful institutions in the current environment are those which have become attractive because their improved control increases profitability.
(d) *A strong home market and business core*: The strengths of the home market and core business are prerequisites for successful enlargement since there is an inevitable period when the basic operation must sustain the growing organisation. Erosion of the 'home base' can seriously impair fundamental soundness, and the expanding bank relies on its basic strengths to generate investor confidence.

(e) *Sound financial condition*: Without a sound balance sheet no institution will be able to convince its investors that their funds are safe; if the institution cannot start out healthy it is unlikely to do well when it expands. The sound financial base is fundamental to investor confidence.

These lessons are being relearned all across Europe today.

Current responses within the EC

The banks of the European Community are already positioning themselves to meet the challenges of the new regime. The most striking response to date has been that of the Deutsche Bank which in 1986 acquired control of the Banca d'America d'Italia. This has given it access to 100 branches servicing medium-sized commercial customers and private clients. Since then it has been trying to acquire control of the Spanish Banco Comercial Transatlantico – a move which drew a hostile response from the Spanish government which has been trying to undo the effects of the prevailing conservatism and protectionism. When Deutsche Bank finally obtains authorisation for control of Banco Comercial it will have access to a ready-made network of branches serving medium-sized industrial and commercial customers.

Meanwhile, some continental European banks have already identified the attractive margins available in the UK retail and medium-sized commercial sectors: using their London-based operations, previously employed in servicing larger commercial clients, they are said to be planning branch networks to access the smaller customer and are lending increasingly to the UK home buyer.

Some European banks are taking a less aggressive route by teaming up with banks from other Member States – such an alliance has been reported between Hambros, Bayerische Vereinsbank, Banco de Bilbao and Instituto Bancario san Paolo di Torino, in which the participants will operate fee-sharing arrangements for the marketing of products and the provision of facilities. The Royal Bank of Scotland and Banco de Santander are going further, developing cross-holdings and reaching agreement on joint acquisitions. The advantages of this approach are that:

(a) the capital investment is minimal;
(b) the risks are considerably lower;
(c) the cost of disengagement is substantially lower;
(d) each institution concentrates on the home market, avoiding

the strain on the management team which can result from acquisition; and

(e) further developments are not impossible, and may be more effective as relationships between the parties develop with experience.

There are two principal disadvantages: the owners of the service 'brand' will enjoy disproportionate longer-term advantages at the expense of those merely delivering the product; and alliances rarely work in practice (witness the decline of the consortium banks which were such a feature of the 1970s).

In response to these developments, governments are initiating changes in their own national markets with the intention of strengthening their banking institutions while they still have time. Spain has already been mentioned: it seems to have put the Deutsche Bank's acquisition on hold in order to permit its multitude of domestic institutions to combine and rationalise themselves into more resilient structures with stronger domestic territories.

Behind the scenes, banks are increasingly joining forces to operate credit cards, automatic teller machines and payment transmission systems. They are moving towards compatible systems so that customers may be serviced using the same cards from virtually any part of the EC. In this they have been encouraged, but not led, by the EC. As the use of EFTPOS increases, the need for compatibility will increase – not least to service the demands of a larger, more mobile and sophisticated customer base with more choices than ever before.

Future developments

The draft Second Banking Directive, with its appended list of permitted activities, seems to envisage the emergence of the 'universal bank' as the predominant force in European banking. Such banks are a natural evolution from the larger German and UK banks which now provide a wide range of banking and financial products. The effect of the proposed legislation will be that these 'universal' banks will be free to market their services throughout the EC – either by cross-border selling, or through branches operating in other Member States. The most obvious market for these entities will be the anticipated 'global corporates' which are expected to emerge over the next few years.

The customer–bank relationship is still of great importance in the selling of banking services. Rather than incur the risks and costs of creating new contact networks it is therefore most likely that the universal banks will either adopt the Deutsche Bank approach, or embark on strategic alliances with less widely-based institutions in order to make their products available in the less advanced markets – which also tend to be those with the most severe restrictions at present, and which are also believed to have the highest assumed potential price differentials.

The main impact of all these developments is likely to be felt in the retail and small to medium commercial sectors – sectors which have been subject to the greatest protection and the most evident oligopoly at national level. Many institutions have highlighted these sectors as important targets, and are already building up capabilities to service these customers through enhanced branch networks. Business for high net-worth individuals also appears to be an attractive prospect and institutions are increasingly targeting such people with a range of up-market value-added products.

As in the United States, wholesale banking has not been subject to such tight controls and it is probable that the current supply of services will be sufficient to meet the demand released by complete liberalisation of the movement of capital. The main issue will be who gains this new business – and again it is likely to be the degree of proximity to those sources which will be a determining factor: thus again it is likely to be the well-prepared 'universal' banks which will benefit. Given London's pre-eminence in this market it is likely that much of the additional business will be serviced from the UK.

There will, however, be areas of the market which the universal banks will find it difficult or uneconomical to service: the most likely reason for this may be a combination of the presence of adequate suppliers with both a depth of experience in relevant products and a strong hold over the local market. This is more likely to be the case for merchant banks or regional banks in developed markets. These institutions may themselves resort to alliances with similar organisations across the continent to enhance their market coverage without compromising on their independence and market base.

Given the current state of the markets, competition will become much more intense and the struggle for growth and market share will redouble. Indeed, it is the Commission's intention to reduce the cost of financial services by increasing competitive pressure. It is therefore inevitable that institutions which do not enjoy financial strength, good core businesses, or competent operational control will either be subsumed into stronger organisations or will simply go out of business. The signs of this are already emerging in Italy and, most notably, in Spain. The UK's building society movement illustrates the point, with a marked tendency for small institutions to be acquired by larger and stronger competitors.

It is clear that whichever course a bank or banks may adopt, the market will be transformed as the consumers of banking products adjust to their enlarged domestic market. The combined effect of harmonisation in all business sectors is likely to put particular emphasis on:

(a) trade finance products and related credit insurance;
(b) foreign exchange;
(c) treasury management, including cross-currency operations; and
(d) information transmission and electronic transfer systems.

With technological developments constantly changing both the possibilities and customer expectations, it is likely that flexibility will become increasingly important – a flexibility in:

(a) the range of services offered,
(b) the types of customers which can be serviced, and
(c) the method of delivering the service.

The above discussion has concentrated on the impact of banking regulation for banks based within the EC. Of equal significance will be the impact on the structure and operations of non-EC banks – particularly those in the powerful financial centres of the United States, Japan and Switzerland. Most of the major banks are already established in Europe in one form or another, either through branches or subsidiaries. The immediate likely impact for non-EC institutions is for them to review their organisational structures and ensure that any reciprocity proposals have limited impact upon their operations. This may mean the transformation of current branch operations into subsidiaries and close consideration of where banking subsidiaries should be established within the EC. While a subsidiary established anywhere within the EC will give the non-EC bank the power to expand throughout the EC, there may be considerable tax and regulatory differences caused by the 'centre' picked within the EC for operations. Non-EC banks will therefore be carefully considering their strategy for Europe to ensure that they are established in the 'right' places to take advantage of the vast European consumer market.

United States and Swiss institutions, particularly, already have a significant presence within Europe. They have also the weight of capital behind them which is likely to make them a winner in any new environment. The Japanese, whilst present in Europe to serve their large Japanese corporate customers, have not made significant inroads into the European consumer retail markets (although they are very significant in lending to major UK corporates). Their initial reaction will be to ensure that the reciprocity provisions do not impact on their business too significantly.

Many large foreign banks are adopting a strategy of establishing in the main financial centres within Europe, London, Frankfurt, Paris, Amsterdam and Milan and only servicing their large corporate customers. These institutions tend to concentrate on the wholesale money markets. This approach is particularly marked with the United States banks' retrenchment to this basic model, and reflects both the caution engendered by current uncertainty and the difficulties experienced by some United States groups in their recently expanded European operations.

THE EFFECT OF THE 1992 REFORMS – STRUCTURE

The European Commission has continued to develop its thinking on the subject of company law within the Community, and although not specifically arrived at the banking sector, developments in this area may have a significant impact. The following developments are of particular interest.

The European Economic Interest Grouping (EEIG)

The intention behind the EEIG is to facilitate cross-frontier corporation for joint ventures in activities which are non-profit making. Research and development, purchasing and general marketing have been mentioned in this context. The legislation creates an entity which is incorporated within Community, rather than national law, obviating many of the difficulties associated with combinations backed by entities from different Member States, each operating under its own legislative framework.

The EEIG is perhaps a natural vehicle for some aspects of the trans-European banking sector: in view of the restriction to non-profit making activities the most likely users may be in the provision of services, such as the operation of funds transfer systems and currency and securities settlement services. Publicity and product development could also be operated within such a structure.

The advantages may be greatest for those institutions which adopt the 'alliance' approach, since they will be able to neutralise the effects of differences in company law, but universal banks may also find the EEIG fulfilling a useful role in similar activities for combinations of branch networks and separately incorporated entities across Europe.

The European Company

The commission has proposed a directive which would create a 'European Company', incorporated and administered under the provision of a distinct Community-level company law. The proposal is regarded as having four principal benefits:

(a) co-operation between enterprises across frontiers would be improved by creating a set of specifically European legal instruments;
(b) the cost and complexity of cross-border restructurings and groupings would be greatly reduced;
(c) legal restrictions on cross-border operations would be alleviated; and
(d) worker-involvement in decision-making would be enhanced.

This proposal would certainly be important for the banking sector in that the move towards 'universal' bank expansion is currently restricted by the legal prohibitions against cross-border mergers. Even if these were permitted, the variations in national requirements would greatly complicate the process. Directives are in hand on specific aspects of the merger problem, but the proposals would transform the basic environment in which corporate structure is determined.

The extent to which banks choose to incorporate as European companies will depend on the relative attraction of the associated legal provisions, but clearly the Commission recognises that the system must be sufficiently attractive to inhibit migration to the most favourable legislative regimes offered by Member States. (It should be noted, however, that the proposal is no soft option by UK standards, although it may seem more attractive to German or Belgian companies.)

It is therefore likely that the directive will offer a degree of flexibility to companies currently incorporated in the Member States. Substantial tax incentives have been suggested – most interestingly, in the form of a right to set branch losses incurred in Member States against branch profits in other Member States.

This area is closely fraught with problems, and any plans which affect national fiscal control will meet such resistance from Member States that the Commission is unlikely to achieve substantial progress in the foreseeable future.

The main attraction for the time being will be that trans-European banks will be able to adopt a corporate structure which avoids the complexities of the diverse national regimes. This may be a distinct advantage when banks examine the impact on their business of regulatory diversity, and banks may be able to reduce their legal and accountancy teams in the long run.

One issue which will doubtless prove unattractive to many institutions will be provisions requiring European companies to allocate seats on the supervisory board to workers' representatives. This is seen by many as interventionist, preventing institutions from operating as they see fit: this view should be considered in the context of the struggles we have witnessed between managers trying to assert their right to manage and workers trying to preserve their vested interests. The Commission is likely to propose a compromise which offers companies a degree of choice in the matter, depending on national custom, but the proposal has a long way to go before implementation, and much could change before then.

Structural impact of regulatory diversity

The acquisition approach suggests that the universal bank is likely to obtain companies in the countries into which it will expand, thereby creating a pan-European group. Likewise the alliance approach is likely to result in legal entities operating within each 'ally's' home nation. However, the regulatory regime post-1992 will still differ between Member States. Moreover, approaches to taxation will continue to vary considerably (with some nations taxing interest and dividends at source, others not imposing withholding tax).

Banks throughout Europe will still be faced with a wide range of regulatory and taxation detail and it is to be expected that the legal structure of their operations will be designed to maximise their commercial opportunities within the various regimes. For example, a bank based (i.e. incorporated) in one Member State may find itself prevented by its home regulator from transacting a class of business anywhere in Europe, whereas competitors based in more liberal states may be providing the services under their home state's authorisation. One solution may be to incorporate a subsidiary in a more permissive Member State (which would be the subsidiary's 'home regulator') and to use that as the vehicle for business not permitted by the parent's home regulator.

The European Company may prove to be a valuable addition to the range of legislative regimes, and as the banks and their professional advisers become more experienced in the mechanics of the regulatory regimes throughout Europe we may find a number of instances where banks take steps to ensure that their legal structure exploits the opportunities.

THE EFFECT OF THE 1992 REFORMS – ACCOUNTS

As with so many aspects of the European banking sector, the accounting disclosure requirements vary considerably from country to country. The Fourth Company Law Directive did not apply to the banking sector, so the situation has not changed in line with the other sectors. Although some central banks have attempted to improve disclosure in their territory by persuasion, the outcome has not led to uniformity, and the use of published accounts for comparing the performance in the sector is therefore difficult and uninformative.

The current situation in Europe can best be illustrated by examples:

Spanish law permits hidden reserves and contains few disclosure requirements. Consolidations are not mandatory and the methods of consolidation vary considerably. There is no formal audit requirement. The central bank has asked banks to produce at least a consolidated balance sheet, profit and loss account and funds flow statement, but the lack of accounting standards seriously limits the value of the information. Window dressing is quite common at reporting period-ends.

Italy applies four basic concepts, but otherwise has no formal principles for the accounting treatment of banking transactions. Hidden reserves are common. There are no requirements for notes to the financial statements, but directors' reports are used to disclose some accounting information, largely at the directors' discretion. The accounts of quoted banks must be audited.

German banks are required to disclose assets and liabilities in order of liquidity, but liquidity is determined by reference to original contract terms rather than known outcomes. Movements in loan provisions are netted off. German banks tend to be extremely prudent in their assessment of asset values.

France now requires notes to the financial statements but does not specify disclosure requirements. Basic concepts are applied, but tax-related treatments influence accounting treatments to a considerable extent. Hidden reserves are common.

This diversity is undesirable *per se* because of the difficulties it presents to users of the financial statements: in many states it would be quite difficult to compare any two institutions, even if both were reporting under the same legislation. These problems are multiplied when national differences are introduced. The banking sector is far too significant to the European economy as a whole for this situation to persist. Additionally, banks which report under less-developed disclosure requirements may be at a disadvantage in the capital markets, as users can be expected to require a compensation for the risks attaching to inadequate information.

Timetable and main implications to the UK

Member States are required to bring the directive into law by 31 December 1990 and provide for implementation in respect of accounts for financial years beginning on or after 1 January 1993. The precise impact of the directive on the requirements for UK banks will only become clear when the implementing legislation is published and it is known which of the options available to Member States is adopted by the UK authorities. At present a consultative paper from the Department of Trade and Industry is awaited.

The directive is effectively supplemental to the Fourth and Seventh Directives and contains an overriding requirement that the accounts give a true and fair view. It prescribes a detailed format for the accounts.

Disclosure requirements

There are a number of disclosure requirements which are in excess of those presently in force in the UK including:

(a) a detailed analysis of profit or loss for the year;
(b) an analysis by maturity of loans to credit institutions and customers and of amounts owed to credit institutions and customers;
(c) details of off-balance sheet items, such as contingent liabilities and commitments;
(d) gross amount of foreign currency assets and liabilities translated into local currency;
(e) a statement of the types of unmatured forward transactions,

indicating whether undertaken for hedging or dealing purposes.

There is a prohibition in the directive on the setting-off of assets and liabilities, although the precise ambit of this requirement is not clear. Depending on the interpretation placed on it, it could mark a significant change from present practice for many banks; for example, advances and deposits to the same customer are at present frequently shown only as a single net amount in the balance sheet if there is a legal right of set-off.

Undisclosed reserves
The directive does not permit the creation or use of undisclosed reserves, although there is an option available to Member States to permit assets to be stated at up to 4% below the lower of cost and market value. Movements in this 'value adjustment' are required to be shown separately in the profit and loss account. However, Member States also have the option of permitting the creation of a fund for general banking risks, but the net increase or decrease in this fund must be shown separately in the profit and loss account.

Valuation rules
The directive prescribes valuation rules for various classes of assets which are summarised below.

Intangible and tangible fixed assets must be carried at or below purchase price, unless Member States permit a revaluation reserve to be created. These rules also apply to other assets intended for use on a continuing basis in the normal course of activities, including shares in associated companies and trade investments.

Debt securities held for the long term (that is, investment securities) must be stated at purchase price but Member States may permit or require the amount repayable at maturity to be shown on the balance sheet with the difference charged to profit or released to income in instalments up to maturity. The difference is to be shown separately in the balance sheet or notes.

Loans and advances, debt securities and shares and other variable yield securities not held for the long term must be stated in accordance with the principle of lower of cost and market value.

Foreign currency translation
Assets and liabilities in a foreign currency are to be translated at rates of exchange ruling on the balance sheet date. Member States may however require or permit non-monetary assets to be translated at the rates ruling on the dates of acquisition.

Spot exchange transactions must be translated at spot rates of exchange on the balance sheet date. Uncompleted forward exchange transactions are also to be translated at spot rates of forward exchange unless Member States provide that they are being translated at forward rates.

Differences on translation must be included in the profit and loss account. However, Member States may permit or require the difference relating to non-monetary assets together with transactions undertaken to cover those assets to be included, in whole or in part, in reserves not available for distribution. Member States may also provide that profits arising from the translation of uncovered forward transactions, assets or liabilities are not to be included in the profit and loss account.

The directive permits Member States to require translation differences arising from the translation of overseas operations into the reporting currency to be taken directly to reserves. The use of average rates to translate income or expenditure of affiliates may also be required or permitted.

Conclusion

The directive will lead to significant improvements in the standards of disclosure and presentation required of banks throughout the EC. The users of banks' financial statements will at last have the opportunity to compare the results and financial condition of banks based in different jurisdictions, and will have greater assurance that accounting treatments are consistent from year to year. The vexed question of provisioning will be more readily addressed by the new disclosure and valuation rules in this area.

Analysts and the public will achieve a better understanding of the European banking sector – to the benefit both of themselves and the banking sector.

CONCLUSIONS AND PREDICTIONS

(a) The European market is characterised by diverse regulation and culture, and is therefore extremely fragmented. Previous initiatives to free the market in banking services have had only limited impact.

(b) Regulatory changes *per se* are not the driving force behind change in the industry's reaction to Europe. It is perceptions which have changed – thanks to the awareness campaigns of both the European Commission and national governments.

(c) Research indicates that the costs of comparable financial transactions vary significantly among EC member states. Removal of national barriers within the Community's markets should have a substantial commercial impact – hopefully in reduced prices and greater choice for the consumer.

(d) The impact of market changes will mostly be felt in the retail sector: few changes are likely in wholesale business, though London is likely to benefit from the freedom of capital movements.

(d) Experience in the United States of deregulated retail banking suggests that agreed mergers and acquisitions are the most likely consequence of the 1992 reforms. Success will depend on financial and managerial strength. There will be losers, particularly among the smaller regional retail organisations.

(f) Universal banks will emerge as the main beneficiaries.

(g) Cross-border provision of retail services is unlikely to develop. Service delivery will continue to depend on proximity to the customer base. Relationship banking is certainly neither dead nor dying.

(h) Reciprocity is unlikely to present major obstacles for the determined non-EC institutions, particularly those from Switzerland, the United States and Japan.

(i) Taxation and remaining regulatory differences will continue to influence decisions on location. There is little short-term prospect of taxation harmony.

(j) The 'European Company' is a fairly distant prospect, but may eventually be the ideal vehicle for the true universal bank.

(k) Accounting disclosure will be standardised and will produce improvements throughout the EC. Banks and their investors will benefit.

3—BANKING REGULATION AND 1992

Paul Tillett

INTRODUCTION

The 1980s, as has often been remarked, has witnessed a somewhat paradoxical mixture of deregulation and intensified regulation in financial markets. The trend towards deregulation has been most apparent in the dismantling of restrictions (whether legal restrictions or cartelised practices) which tended to confine the roles of different categories of institution to particular areas of business. There has also been a move away from reliance on direct controls on financial institutions (especially banks) in favour of more market-orientated methods of exercising monetary control. On the other side of the coin have been the moves towards international harmonisation of prudential regulation, which have involved stricter standards for banks in many countries, although not perhaps so much in the UK. At the same time the UK has been in the vanguard of a trend towards the intensification of conduct of business regulation; so far this has been aimed at investment business and has not struck at core banking business.

The Community's 1992 programme for banking and investment services reinforces these divergent tendencies. The Second Banking Directive, by opening up restricted markets, will put pressure on the remaining controls on banks' permitted activities. It may do the same for direct monetary controls, where these survive. Its two accompanying directives, the Own Fund Directive and the Solvency Ratio Directive, will give legal effect in the Community to the agreed international harmonisation of capital adequacy regulation. Meanwhile the Investment Services Directive, which is also likely to be accompanied by one or more capital adequacy directives, will open up investment markets and will involve harmonisation and – in many countries – intensification of prudential regulation for investment business.

In the field of conduct of business regulation, the Investment Services Directive merely scratches at the surface. Like the Second

Banking Directive, it has little to offer in this area but unanswered questions. A Community regime for conduct of business regulation, both in banking and investment business, is a task for the 1990s, but will almost inevitably involve an intensification of regulation in many areas.

The succeeding four sections of this chapter review the four different types of regulation here identified: prudential regulation, the range of permitted activities, monetary controls, and conduct of business regulation. The concluding section summarises the stage the Community has now reached, focusing on the division of responsibility between home and host states.

PRUDENTIAL REGULATION

The aim of the Second Banking Directive – and the two capital adequacy directives that are being pursued in tandem with it – is to provide freedom of establishment and freedom of services in banking on the basis of home country control, having achieved a sufficient degree of regulatory harmonisation to permit the mutual recognition by each Member State of each other's system of control.

A small start was made on the task of harmonising the prudential regulation of banking by the First Banking Directive, adopted by the Council in 1977. This requires every Member State to have a system of prior authorisation for 'credit institutions'. The criteria for authorisation have to include as a minimum four specified elements: the institution must have separate capital (separate, that is, from the resources of its proprietors); it must meet an initial capital requirement (the directive does not say how much); at least two persons must effectively direct its business; and those persons must be of 'sufficient repute' and possess 'sufficient experience'.

The directive also provides for cooperation between supervisors in various areas, but because it still leaves scope for major divergence in supervisory law and practice it does not provide the basis for complete reliance on home country control. All 12 Member States continue to apply their own authorisation requirements to branches of banks from other Member States.

The draft Second Banking Directive fills in a number of the gaps left by the First Directive. For example, a figure (5 million ECU) is supplied for the initial capital requirement. More controversially, a minimum capital requirement of the same amount applying on a continuing basis after authorisation is proposed. The rationale for this is obscure. A capital requirement of a minimum absolute amount applied at the point of authorisation is widely considered to be useful as a means of ensuring that a new bank has sufficient resources to establish the infrastructure of its business and to tide itself over any initial losses. Once the bank is established, however, the need is for its capital to be sufficient to underpin the level of business it actually undertakes. This is supervised in quantitative terms by calculating a solvency ratio, and there seems to be no good reason why there should be a requirement to maintain an absolute minimum amount as well.

The Commission had originally intended to flesh out the requirements relating to the fitness and propriety of managers. In the event, this has not been pursued, perhaps advisably: this seems to be an area best left to the discretion of individual supervisory authorities. However, these are new provisions dealing with the fitness and propriety of substantial shareholders. There is also a controversial article on banks' participations in non-financial businesses (discussed in the section on range of services on p. 51) and a reference to the supervision of banks' administrative and accounting procedures and control mechanisms.

Solvency ratios

More substantial progress towards harmonising prudential regulation is apparent in the two companion proposals, the Own Funds Directive and the Solvency Ratio Directive. Between them they harmonise the ratio calculation against which capital adequacy is appraised: the former specifies the definition of bank capital which constitutes the numerator of the ratio; the latter specifies the weightings to be given to the various assets and off-balance sheet items when constituting the denominator, and lays down a minimum required ratio of 8%.

The details are still under discussion, but the broad effect of the directives will be to give legal effect in the Community to the agreement on the convergence of capital adequacy supervision reached by supervisors in the Group of Ten countries in Basle in June 1988.

The Basle Agreement is undoubtedly a diplomatic triumph, without which the path to harmonisation within the Community would have been immeasurably more difficult. It represents a big step towards the elusive 'level playing field' for which practitioners yearn. It has been particularly well received in the UK, where banks have long felt themselves to be at a competitive disadvantage where capital adequacy is concerned, and where the changes needed to supervisory practice will be less far-reaching than in many other countries.

In some ways this is paradoxical, because in 1973 UK interests were in the vanguard of the opposition to an attempt by the Commission to develop a not altogether dissimilar scheme for a harmonised capital ratio. The opposition sprang from a reluctance to see the flexible system of supervision practised in the UK – whereby each institution's capital needs were judged in relation to its individual circumstances – jeopardised by the implantation of normative ratio controls. In the intervening 15 years, the Bank of England's reliance on ratio calculations has greatly increased, but it remains the case that the supervisor's obligation under the Banking Act is to make a judgment as to whether each individual bank's capital is adequate: the ratios are merely a tool that assists in making that judgment.

In the writer's view, the arguments against excessive reliance on ratio controls are as valid now as they were in 1973. There is in fact no sound theoretical basis for the supposition that the riskiness of a bank's business can be gauged with any degree of accuracy by a ratio of capital to weighted risk assets, not least because of the critical importance of the quality of the assets, as opposed to their quantity, and of the degree to which the portfolio is diversified. The ratio should therefore be a starting point for an assessment of a bank's capital needs, not the end point.

An important feature of the proposals is that the 8% mandatory ratio is a minimum, with supervisors free to set a higher ratio in individual cases. This will allow scope for a judgmental element to be retained. The Bank of England has indicated that nearly all UK banks will be expected to adhere to a higher ratio, but some other EC countries seem to be planning to apply the 8% across the board. In the UK, even though a discretionary element is to be retained, the mandatory ratio will probably have to be given statutory expression, while presumably retaining the overriding requirement that capital must be adequate taking all relevant factors into account. In any event, the directive will further entrench the role of ratios in the supervisory process.

The point should also be made that harmonising capital ratios cannot of itself equalise competitive conditions. Competitive equality would require that the return on capital, not the capital requirement, be equal for the same business transacted by different banks. That cannot be achieved without harmonising the Member States' corporation tax systems as well.

Position risk

A further weakness of the Basle Agreement and of the Solvency Ratio Directive is that the standardised ratio calculation addresses only the credit risk attaching to the various assets and off-balance sheet items. Clearly no banking supervisor can afford to ignore the presence of the many other risks to which a bank is subject. It must therefore be inferred that the choice of the 8% minimum ratio is intended to make allowance, in a crude way, for the presence of these other risks. Variations from one bank to another in the relative extent of these other risks can in principle be allowed for by judgmental variation in the required ratio. But the fact that some supervisory authorities appear not to be planning to vary the ratio in this way inevitably creates pressures to develop a more complicated and all-embracing ratio requirement.

It is of course a delusion to suppose that all the different types of banking risk can ever be reduced to arithmetical measurement, but there is already strong pressure to address the particular subject of position risk. Non-bank security firms and their regulators feel that there will be serious competitive distortions if banks are not subjected to explicit capital requirements in relation to securities positions.

The Second Banking Directive contains an unsatisfactory provision enabling *host* states to impose such requirements. This cuts across the principle of home country control and seems unlikely to survive the directive's passage. The Investment Services Directive, on the other hand, makes capital adequacy exclusively a home state responsibility. In particular, home states must require both banks and non-banks to make 'sufficient provision against market risk', in accordance with a separate directive.

Work on this accompanying directive is at a very early stage. In the case of non-banks, the requirements will no doubt draw on what is already in place in the UK under the Financial Services Act, although there may well be pressures to devise something rather less complicated. In the case of banks, the task is more difficult because position risk attaching to securities held for dealing cannot logically be isolated from the market risk applying to investment securities and, more generally, to the interest rate risk which arises from mismatches between the maturity structure of assets and liabilities. The subject of interest rate risk has been under discussion among banking supervisors for some years, but little consensus seems to have emerged on how it should be handled, or even on whether it should be treated explicitly at all. For most banks, interest rate risk and position risk are but a small part of their overall exposure to risk; the likelihood of their getting into serious difficulties on this account is slight and the topic has consequently not been high on the agenda of most banking supervisors. It remains to be seen whether the Commission will be successful in drafting measures which are conceptually sound and compatible with both the existing solvency ratio proposal and the measures to be applied to non-banks.

Even for non-banks, where the need for explicit capital cover for securities positions is more evident, the subject does not seem to attract the same interest in other Community countries as it does in the UK. Progress on the position risk directive is therefore likely to be slow, and it may well have the effect of delaying the implementation of the Investment Services Directive itself.

Liquidity

For non-banks, a position risk requirement can be used to ensure the firm's liquidity as well as its solvency, and the Financial Services Act rules in the UK are designed to achieve this. For banks, on the other hand, the supervision of liquidity is a separate matter from capital adequacy, and requires monitoring of banks' prospective cash flows, their stock of liquid assets and their access to market sources of deposits.

The draft Second Banking Directive gives responsibility for the supervision of liquidity to the *host* state. This will almost certainly be changed to make it clear that the host state only has this responsibility in relation to branches (not cross-border business), and then only in conjunction with the home state. Host state responsibility for liquidity is in accordance with agreements among the Basle group of banking supervisors, but it has become controversial in the UK, where the Bank of England is endeavouring to develop a more prescriptive system for supervising the stock of liquid assets held by banks. The recitals of the Second Banking Directive foreshadow future work on the harmonisation of the supervision of liquidity, with a view to eventual home country control. This will not be an easy task.

RANGE OF SERVICES

Community banking legislation applies to 'credit institutions', defined as undertakings 'whose business is to receive deposits and other repayable funds from the public and to grant credits for its own account'. Thus it is the two core banking services of deposit taking and lending that determine the ambit of the scheme of prudential regulation and which qualify undertakings for the 'passport' which gives them freedom of establishment and freedom of services.

However, it would obviously be unsatisfactory if the Treaty

freedoms extended to the provision of these two services alone. Banks almost invariably complement them with a range of ancillary services which they would also wish to provide outside their home state. In some countries, the range of services permitted to banks is laid down in legislation; in others it is regulated solely through the supervisory process. The UK adopts the latter approach for banks, but the former for building societies.

One solution would have been to harmonise the permitted range of services at Community level. This course would almost certainly have encountered implacable opposition, and seems never to have been seriously entertained. Instead, with one possible exception noted below, the proposed Second Directive settles for mutual recognition of each Member State's arrangements for controlling the range of services a bank may offer. At the same time, the scope of the 'passport' is limited by reference to a list of banking services annexed to the directive. A bank may then provide any service on the list into another Member State, provided that its home-state authorisation permits the activity.

It is presumably not necessary that the home-state authorisation should *expressly permit* the activity in question. In order to accommodate the position in countries whose banking legislation does not constrain the range of services, the 'passport' needs to apply to activities *not prohibited* by the home state: this needs to be clarified when the text is revised. There is a question mark over services which are not prohibited under the home state's banking legislation, but which cannot in fact be provided without a separate authorisation under some other piece of legislation. For example, in the UK a bank may provide any service so far as the Banking Act is concerned – so long as it continues to fulfil the prudential criteria – but it cannot engage in securities business (a listed activity under the directive) unless it is authorised to do so under the Financial Services Act. It would be reasonable to deny the 'passport' to services for which a bank needs, but does not possess, specific authorisation in its home state.

It may be that the reference to services being 'permitted' does achieve this. The Investment Services Directive uses slightly different terminology. It makes banks exempt from the requirement to obtain authorisation under that directive for investment business activities in so far as its authorisation under the banking directives 'includes the activity in question'. It should be noted that the general approach of the Investment Services Directive to the range of permitted activities is different. It too has annexed to it a list of services, of which most, if not all, are included in the Second Banking Directive list. But whereas the Second Banking Directive list is no more than an attempt to specify the services considered sufficiently integral to banking to warrant being covered by the passport, in the Investment Services Directive the annex is a list of discrete services (for example, 'market making', 'portfolio management', 'brokerage') each of which would require specific authorisation in its own right. This is in fact not inconsistent with the approach of the Financial Services Act, under which an authorised firm is authorised only for particular activities, namely those included in its approved 'business plan'.

The Second Banking Directive's approach of divorcing the scope of the 'passport' from the ambit of regulation therefore causes untidiness at the interface with the Investment Services Directive. A more serious problem, perhaps, is the violence it does to competitive neutrality. Banks based in countries which allow them to carry out a wide range of services will be at some competitive advantage relative to those where the range of permitted services is narrow. The hope is that, under the threat of the competition likely to be offered by banks from outside, restrictionist countries will see their way to abolishing those restraints on their banks which other countries find unnecessary. This is a good example of the Commission's policy of achieving the single market through the operation of market forces as well as by means of legislative harmonisation.

It is, however, a matter for speculation how far national governments will in the event prove responsive to such pressures. One would be more confident were it not that the Second Directive appears to leave restrictionist countries considerable licence to impede the provision of services by banks from outside. As is discussed later in this chapter, while host states must in principle allow banks from outside to provide listed services in their territory, they can nevertheless regulate the way the services are carried out, so long as the legal provisions in question are 'justified on the grounds of the public good'. The distinction between preventing a service from being provided and preventing it from being provided in a certain way may sometimes be tenuous. Every financial service rests, in the last analysis, on a contract (express or implied) between the institution and its customers, governed by the law of the host state and enforceable only in so far as its provisions are in conformity with the host state's public policy.

To give two examples: some countries prohibit the payment of interest on sight deposits, and some prohibit variable-rate mortgages. Are interest-bearing sight deposits and variable-rate mortgages services in their own right, or merely ways of providing a service? Both are fundamental to the operation of British building societies, and the Treaty freedoms can have little meaning for the societies if the 'public good' provisions can be used to disallow them.

It may be that it will be left to the Court of Justice to determine the extent of the freedoms the Second Directive confers. As discussed later, there are grounds for optimism that the court will in fact grant host states only limited scope for 'public good' restrictions. Nevertheless, having to rely on the court is not very satisfactory. Not only can the process take a long time, but banks may be reluctant to risk testing the validity of a host state's legislation if the consequence may be that its contracts are unenforceable.

There is a case therefore for saying that the directive ought to be more specific as to what is intended. It is noteworthy that the Commission has not yet abandoned the proposed Mortgage Credit Directive, which would specify 'financial techniques' that host states would be required to tolerate, even though mortgage credit is included in the Second Banking Directive list. However, the difficulties of drafting such provisions even for mortgage credit, let alone the whole range of banking services, are enormous and it seems unlikely that this route will be followed. All the same, it would be helpful if clearer understandings could be developed between the Member States as to how the 'passport' and the 'public good' provisions are meant to interrelate.

Participations

The area where the provisions of the Second Directive do seek to harmonise curbs on the range of a bank's activities is that of participations, by which is meant shareholdings in subsidiary and associated companies. It is proposed to place limits on banks' participations in companies which are not themselves banks or financial institutions. The limits are expressed as percentages of the bank's own capital.

No satisfactory explanation has been adduced for including these controls in the directive; several Member States do not currently find them necessary. They may be intended partly as a prudential control, but it is not clear why this aspect cannot be handled through the solvency ratio calculation.

The proposals are misconceived, not least because they attack only one particular form of corporate organisation, that in which non-financial activities are hived down to subsidiary companies owned by the bank. If the non-financial activities are carried on by the bank itself, or if the bank and the non-financial companies are subsidiaries of a common holding company, the directive does not bite at all on the extent of the non-financial activities.

MONETARY CONTROL

When discussing the monetary management of the economy, economists are usually careful to distinguish between the *targets* of monetary policy – the proximate targets, such as the configuration of exchange rates and interest rates and the size of the money stock, and the ultimate targets of growth, employment and other factors of economic well-being – and the *instruments* of monetary control whereby these targets are secured. The instruments may include open market operations on the part of the central bank, or controls placed upon commercial banks, such as compulsory reserve ratios, restrictions on interest rates paid or received or controls on the volume of lending.

The Commission has tended to focus on the generalities of monetary policy, with its vision of a common currency and a Community central bank, and to neglect the nuts and bolts of monetary control which are of day-to-day importance to banks. The Second Banking Directive misses an opportunity here. The Treaty does not remove Member States' exclusive competence in respect of the targets of monetary policy, but it does not automatically follow that Member States must have complete autonomy in respect of the deployment of the instruments of control.

Since monetary controls on banks are going out of fashion in many countries, one might have hoped to see progress by 1992 towards eliminating burdensome and unnecessary controls in those countries that still retain them. At the very least, the directive could remain silent on the point, requiring such controls to be 'justified on the grounds of the public good' if they are to be retained. Instead, the Commission's text expressly reserves to host states control over 'measures resulting from the implementation of monetary policy'. As drafted, it does this not only for branches but also for cross-border business, which would surely be unworkable.

A particular problem here is that some controls are imposed on banks partly for monetary reasons and partly for other reasons (for the supervision of liquidity, for example, or as a selective credit control, or as a disguised tax). If the position is that a host state can impose any control – on cross-border business as well as on branches – which it claims is for monetary purposes, the effect is likely to be to further inhibit the opening up of markets. The example cited in the previous section of a prohibition on paying interest on sight deposits is one which could be represented as a monetary control.

The directive does say that monetary controls must not be imposed on non-domestic banks in a discriminatory way. But this does not dispose of the problem. In some countries, certain markets have remained undeveloped because of the way controls have stifled the activities of the domestic banks. It is in just such areas that banks from elsewhere might expect to benefit from the 1992 programme.

Exchange controls

A related issue concerns restrictions on capital movements. Sometimes these take the form of prohibiting residents from establishing an account relationship with non-domestic banks. It goes without saying that the removal of such restrictions is an essential prerequisite of a common market in banking. The capital movements directives adopted by the Council in June 1988 will abolish all restrictions on capital movements, albeit only after a disappointingly long transitional period in some countries, and only subject to a safeguard clause enabling them to be reintroduced in case of need. The hope is that once exchange controls have been removed, restrictionist countries will find direct controls on banks unworkable and abolish them, as occurred in the UK after 1979.

The removal of exchange controls also prompts questions about the effects of the tax system on cross-border banking business. Fears have been expressed that the ability to place deposits in banks in other countries will lead to widespread tax evasion. In February 1989 the Commission issued a proposal for a harmonised withholding tax on interest payments, applying both to securities and to bank deposits, although with an exemption for eurobonds. It is not clear, however, that the risk of widespread evasion is a real one. Nor is it clear, if there is such a problem, that a Community withholding tax is a solution: tax evaders may simply transfer their money outside the Community altogether.

Attention also needs to be paid to the impact of withholding taxes on bank lending. Where the recipient of a cross-border bank loan is required to withhold tax from the interest (as in Belgium), and where the lending bank in unable to obtain full relief for the tax withheld (as in the UK), the effect can be to make the transaction completely uneconomic. In this way the tax system could continue to thwart cross-border business after the Second Banking Directive and the capital movements directive have removed the other obstacles. Arguably, a tax provision of this sort which undermines the freedom of services is illegal, especially perhaps if it involves discrimination against non-domestic lenders, but it does seem that Commission initiatives in the field of corporation tax are a necessary element in building the single market.

CONDUCT OF BUSINESS REGULATION

The Second Banking Directive says nothing explicit about the regulation of conduct of business. It leaves the way clear to host countries to impose such regulation as they think fit, so long as the rules in question are 'justified on the grounds of the public good'. In avoiding the subject, the directive mirrors the position under the banking legislation of many Member States. Indeed, conduct of business regulation has not hitherto been a live issue at all in relation to banking. The UK Banking Act merely says that a bank's business must be carried on with 'integrity', and there is no corpus of regulation or systematic supervisory procedures designed to enforce that requirement.

Banks are within the scope of consumer credit legislation, both Community and domestic, but apart from that it is in the investment field that conduct of business regulation is to the fore. Even here, it is primarily in the UK that the subject is a live one. Certain other Member States are showing hesitant signs of following the UK lead, but in others the concept seems to be barely understood.

It had earlier been thought that the Commission's work on the Investment Services Directive would bring the subject to a head in the Community context. It was always accepted that, because of the great diversity of approaches in different countries to the regulation of investment business, it would be impossible to move straight to a system of home country control, and that large areas of conduct of business regulation would at this stage continue to be the responsibility of the host state. UK interests in particular were keen that as much regulation as possible should rest with the host state, because of understandable fears that the home country control exercised by most other Member States would continue to be less stringent than that in place in the UK.

In the event, the Commission's proposal provides for home country control only for those aspects that concern the structure of the firm itself, such as the control of conflicts of interest ('Chinese walls') and the segregation of client's assets from those of the firm. These are really concomitants of the general requirement that firms be 'fit and proper', a matter that only the home country authorities are in a position to judge. They could be said to fall into the same general category as the requirement, laid down in the same article of the directive, that the home state must make rules governing 'sound administrative and accounting procedures and internal control mechanisms'. Other home state responsibilities specified relate to membership of compensation schemes (which may prove controversial) and to record-keeping and the provision of information (which are surely an inevitable feature of any system of regulation, and are presumably not intended to exclude corresponding requirements imposed by host states to back up their rules).

Some of the Commission's early drafts contained a parallel article listing a number of areas in which host states would have been required to make rules. In the eventual proposal this has all been deleted. Thus, not only is responsibility for most conduct of business regulation left to the host state, but there is no attempt at all at harmonising the way host states discharge their responsibility. The only proviso is that the rules must be 'justified on the grounds of the public good', the same formulation as in the Second Banking Directive.

This is something of an admission of defeat so far as achieving a single market is concerned, but a slimmed-down directive of this sort does stand a much greater chance of acceptance by 1992, giving non-bank investments businesses the same 'passport' rights in their own fields as those enjoyed by banks. The approach also has the merit of being consistent with the Second Banking Directive in essentially leaving conduct of business regulation on one side. The way is thus clear for the subject to be addressed simultaneously both for banking and investment business in the next phase of the Community's development. The light conduct of business regime currently enjoyed by banks for 'banking' business not subject to the Financial Services Act may then become a thing of the past. Equally, one hopes that the heavy-handed regime of that Act for investment business will be ameliorated by the process of Community harmonisation.

In the meantime, the question arises as to what constraints Community law places on the systems of conduct of business regulation established by host states. First, it may be noted in passing that in countries such as the UK, where the regulatory tasks are entrusted in part to professional associations voluntarily formed by practitioners, the rules may be open to challenge under art. 85 of the Treaty if they have the effect of distorting competition. It is likely that problems on this score were influential in the decision in the UK to abandon rules constraining the commissions paid to brokers by life assurance and unit trust companies, which had been intended to buttress the requirement for brokers to give 'best advice'.

The 'public good'

That complication apart, the key question is how the court will interpret the words 'justified on the grounds of the public good'. This is discussed more fully in other chapters. The concept of the 'public good' can be traced back to the jurisprudence of the court in cases concerned with the free movement of goods, of which the best known is *Cassis de Dijon*.[1] This case established that any national legislation which is capable of hindering, directly or indirectly, actually or potentially, intra-Community trade is deemed equivalent to a quantitative restriction and is therefore potentially illegal under art. 30 of the Treaty. Restrictions may be maintained only if they are used to promote legitimate objectives of policy, and only if they are in proportion to those objectives: such barriers to trade as may be permitted can only go so far as is necessary for the reasonable purposes for which they have been introduced.

Two of the policy objectives found by the court to be legitimate are consumer protection and fair trading practices. Extrapolating from the general principles established for the free movement of goods, it seems certain that, if called upon to do so, the court would find investor protection to be a legitimate objective where private investors are concerned, but it is not clear that rules impinging on dealings with professional or business investors would necessarily be upheld. Rules which were not absolutely necessary to secure adequate protection could still fail the proportionality test, in particular rules which are unnecessary by reason of the fact that they duplicated regulation imposed in the home state. Rules considered necessary in some Member States but not in others might be regarded as particularly vulnerable. The example cited earlier of a prohibition on variable-rate mortgages could be a likely case in point.

Some further light is cast by the judgments of the court in the four insurance cases in December 1986.[2] Because they deal with services rather than goods, they are closer to home. They were, however, concerned only with cross-border services, not with business carried out through branches.

1. Case 120/78 *Rewe Zentrale AG* v *Bundesmonopolverwaltung für Branntwein* [1979] ECR 649.
2. See J Flynn, 'Insurance: Recent Judgments of the European Court of Justice' (1988) 37 ICLQ 154.

The court confirmed that in 'sensitive' areas, such as insurance, host states were entitled to impose their own rules with regard to matters where a Community legislative framework had not been achieved. These rules, however, had to be objectively justified by reference to the public interest or 'general good', which encompassed consumer protection, and the rules also had to be appropriate for the purpose they were designed to achieve. In addition, the host state would need to apply the rules to its own nationals, and would also have to take into account any equivalent rules which were applied in the home state (in particular host states should not duplicate such rules).

In the case of services included in the lists annexed to the Second Banking Directive and the Investment Services Directive, an element of confusion arises from the fact that one of the court's tests is whether the matter is covered by a directive. In a sense, the regulation of listed services is covered by the directives, if only to say that host state rules are enforceable only to the extent that they are 'justified on the grounds of the public good'. Is this test meant to be the same as that developed by the court, or is it a different one? Presumably it is the same, though it is puzzling that the directive refers to the 'public good' rather than the 'general good'. In the case of investment services, it seems clear that the host state regulation cannot duplicate the areas of home state regulation specified in the directive, and it is probable that it must not duplicate any further regulation the home state may choose to impose outside the framework of the directive. This suggests that it would be helpful if, as well as specifying rules that must be imposed by home states, the directive were to indicate areas where home states should refrain from making rules that bite on cross-border business so that the way is left clear for host states to make the rules.

It is also noteworthy that, in the insurance judgments, the court drew a distinction between risks underwritten for consumers and the risks of substantial businesses, the latter customers being considered not to need the degree of protection found to be justified for consumers. This lends further support to the view that host states may have only limited scope for applying rules to banks or investment firms governing their dealings with non-personal customers.

CONCLUSION

The prime objectives of the current phase of Community legislation affecting the regulation of banks is to establish a system of home country control, with sufficient harmonisation to allow the mutual recognition of each Member State's method of exercising control. The extent of the progess made can therefore conveniently be summarised by reviewing the regulatory division of labour between home and host states provided for by the directives currently under negotiation.

Of the four types of regulation described in this chapter, progress has been most apparent in the regulation of the range of permitted services. The home state is responsible for deciding which services may be offered, and if those services are included in the list annexed to the relevant directive they may be provided throughout the Community. The only exception concerns the unsatisfactory controls in the Second Banking Directive on banks' 'participations' in non-financial companies.

In the field of prudential regulation, matters are also well advanced. If the reference in the Second Banking Directive to host state control of 'provisions against market risk' is no more than an aberration, home country control is in principle achieved for the supervision of capital adequacy. It still remains to be achieved for the supervision of bank liquidity. It should be emphasised, however, that difficult discussions lie ahead on the harmonisation of capital requirements in relation to 'market risk', both for non-banks and for banks. The point should also be made that the term 'home country control' could be somewhat misleading. The directives rightly give *responsibility* for prudential regulation to the home state. The actual task of monitoring compliance is, in practice, a joint effort between the home and host authorities. At present, the necessary basis for collaboration is more firmly established among banking supervisors than it is among securities supervisors.

One disappointment is that the Second Banking Directive entrenches host state control in the field of monetary controls, by which is meant the deployment of the instruments of monetary policy. While it would not perhaps have been politically realistic to expect host states readily to give up these powers, it would have been perfectly possible for the Second Banking Directive to remain silent on the subject.

The area where most remains to be done is that of conduct of business regulation. In the directives so far proposed, conduct of business regulation is left almost entirely to host states. Nor is any attempt made to harmonise the manner in which host states discharge their role, except that their rules are constrained to an unknown extent by the vague proviso that they must be 'justified on the grounds of the public good'. So far, the degree of consensus as to what is required in this area is weak. Doubts are likely to be expressed as to whether it is right even in principle for some types of conduct of business regulation to be the responsibility of the home state. Aggrieved investors in the host state may wish to make their complaints to their own authorities, and may expect effective action to be taken in that quarter; but it is as yet an open question how far it is possible for conduct of business rules to be laid down by one authority but enforced by another. At all events, the way forward will be fraught with difficulties.

4—RETAIL BANKING SERVICES IN 1992

Marc Dassesse

THE SIGNIFICANCE OF 1992 FOR RETAIL SERVICES

The liberalisation of European financial markets is in the process of being achieved as a result of a number of directives, among which the most important are, for the purposes of this chapter:

(a) The Directive of 24 June 1988 removing restrictions to capital movements;[1]
(b) The proposal for a Second Banking Directive[2]; and
(c) The proposal for an Investment Services Directive.[3]

It is generally accepted that the implementation of the above (draft) directives will affect, primarily, individuals and small-and medium-sized enterprises (SMEs) and not the large multinationals, which already operate in the various Member States. In contrast with such multinationals who have been aware for some considerable time of how to use the divergences existing between the various national financial and fiscal systems to their advantage and which have direct access to the Euromarkets, the SMEs and private individuals have access, in the normal course, only to their national markets as regards both their financial requirements and the investment of their assets and savings.

This continued partitioning of financial markets at the level of retail services, more than 30 years after the signing of the Treaty of Rome, would at first glance seem astonishing. Indeed, the Court

1. Council Directive 88/361/EEC of 24 June 1988 for the implementation of art. 67 of the Treaty: OJ L178/5, 8 July 1988.
2. Proposal for a Second Council Directive on the co-ordination of laws, regulations and administrative provisions relating to the taking up and pursuit of the business of credit institutions amending Directive 77/780/EEC COM (87) 715 final: OJ C84/1, 31 March 1988.
3. Proposal for a Council Directive on investment services in the securities field, COM (88) 778, STN 176: OJ C43/7, 22 February 1989.

of Justice has been insisting for many years, in fact from the end of the transitional period (1 January 1970), that individuals and undertakings could avail themselves directly (even in the face of national legal provisions to the contrary) of the freedom of establishment[4] and of the freedom to provide services[5]. The Court of Justice further declared in this regard that the freedom to provide services included not only the right of the supplier of the service to provide such service to a customer established in another Member State, but also the right of the recipient of the service to go to another Member State in order to receive the service there.[6]

In practice, however, it is only the freedom of establishment which can be effectively exercised throughout the Community at the present time. This has been made possible as a result of the entry into force of the First Banking Directive in 1977.[7] In terms of this directive, it was formally provided that any banking institution of one Member State can establish itself in another Member State by means of setting up a branch there.

This right, however, can only be exercised with the approval of the supervisory authorities of that foreign state (the host country). It should be noted that such approval can only be refused on the basis of the limited and objective criteria laid down in the directive, and not simply at the discretion of those national authorities (for example, if there was a surplus of banking institutions in the local market).

This approach, according to which approval has to be obtained to set up a branch and that such a branch must be supervised by the local national authorities under the same terms and conditions as those applying to banking institutions created in accordance with the law of the host country, has two important consequences:

(a) It results in it being extremely onerous for a bank to set up a branch in another Member State by reason notably of the requirement to allocate (at least in principle) the same endowment capital to the branch as that which is required for the locally incorporated banks;
(b) It requires the branch so set up to comply, both in its relations with the local supervisory authorities and with its local

4. *Reyners, Jean* v *Belgian State*, Case 2/74, 21 June 1974, [1974] ECR 631.
5. *Van Binsbergen* v *Bestuur van de Bedrijfsvereniging Voor de Metaalnijverheid*, Case 37/74, 31 December 1974, [1974] ECR 1299.
6. *Luisi and Carbone* v *Ministero del Tesoro* joined cases 286/82 and 26/83, 31 January 1984, [1984] ECR 377.
7. First Banking Co-ordination Directive (77/780/EEC), OJ L322/30, 17 December 1977.

> customers, with the various national regulations applicable to the local banking institutions. Therefore, the branch is not able to benefit from any competitive advantages that it may have as the result of a more flexible regulatory system applicable in the country of origin (home country), especially as regards 'financial techniques' (such as, for example, the use of variable interest rates for mortgage credits, which is banned in some countries and allowed in others).

As a result, branches opened in one Member State by a bank of another Member State have been geared, as a general rule, to wholesale banking operations and not to the servicing of the local clientele of private individuals and SMEs.

In the area of the freedom to provide services, it must be noted that, in general, such a freedom has not extended to the area of retail services. In this sector, the exercise of this freedom has met with three sets of obstacles.

First, there still exist exchange regulations in certain Member States which prohibit individuals or undertakings from freely transferring or holding financial assets which are not directly related to the exercise of commercial operations concerning imports or exports. The Court of Justice, in fact, considered this issue in its judgment of 11 November 1981 in the *Casati* case, where it held that the free movement of capital and of current payments provided for in art. 67 of the Treaty were not producive of direct effect:[8] therefore, individuals and undertakings can only avail themselves of these provisions to the extent that these freedoms have been implemented in terms of directly applicable directives adopted by the Council. An exception to this rule exists with regard to art. 106 of the Treaty when the free movement of capital and of current payments are exercised as a corollary to the implementation of one of the four fundamental freedoms (free movement of goods and persons, freedom of establishment and the freedom to provide services) which are already fully in force. Thus, for example, the freedom to provide services involves, as an essential corollary, the right of the purchaser to render payment to the seller, and to acquire for this purpose the necessary currency.[9]

Secondly, various national regulations with a view to consumer protection and in the interests of general public policy, frequently involve a prohibition on foreigners soliciting investment business, selling financial services and/or supplying credit unless they have

8. *Casati, Geurrino*, Case 203/80, 11 November 1981, [1981] ECR 2595.
9. See footnote 6.

received prior approval from the authorities of the host country. In practice, this approval presupposes necessarily the existence of a branch in that Member State where the interested party seeks to exercise the freedom to provide services (host country).

Finally, local fiscal regulations often constitute an obstacle to the freedom to provide financial services. For example, the grant of credit facilities by a bank established in one Member State to an individual or an undertaking resident in another Member State is generally rendered impossible where the individual or undertaking is required to retain a withholding tax on the interest paid to the foreign bank. In addition, numerous fiscal provisions tend to favour certain types of credit (for example, mortgage loans) or certain types of investments where these are arranged by local lenders or the investment is effected in local financial assets (a more detailed analysis of this subject follows on p. 84–9).

RECENT DECISIONS OF THE COURT OF JUSTICE AND DIRECTIVES

Developments involving branches: home country control and abolition of the endowment capital requirement

The Second Banking Directive has widely adopted the principle of home country control. In general, this means that the various supervisory functions to be exercised over a bank's activities, including the activities of its branches in the other Member States, will fall to the authorities of the Member State where the bank has its head office.

The supervisory authorities of that Member State where the branch is set up will retain competence only with respect to the supervising of liquidity and the monitoring of monetary policy.[10] Therefore, the authorities of the host country lose all competence over solvency regulation.

This transfer of competence from the authorities of the host country is made possible by the proposed simultaneous entry into

10. In the present draft of the proposal for a Second Banking Directive, the supervisory authorities of the host country retain competence with regard to the risks arising out of the trading of securities within their territory. It is understood, however, that this issue will be the subject of a separate directive and that the text of the banking directive, when adopted, will reflect a modification of this provision.

force, along with the Second Banking Directive, of Community directives concerning Solvency Ratios[11] and Own Funds[12]. In tandem with the above measures, the Commission has indicated that it reserves the right, if necessary, to translate into the form of directives, its recommendations on large risk exposure[13] and deposit guarantee schemes[14].

The power of the authorities of the host country to require certain minimum levels of endowment capital for such branches of foreign banks has been removed. Existing branches will therefore regain control of their endowment capital from the entry into force of the directive.

Currently, the Second Banking Directive does provide that the authorities of the home country must establish a minimum capital requirement of at least 5 million ECU (as a rule) for its banks.

However, the Second Banking Directive expressly allows the authorities of the home country to set a higher capital threshold. But such authorities cannot seek to oppose the setting up in their territory of branches of banks having their head office in another Member State in which Member State only the minimum capital as provided for by the directive is required. Consider the following example: if the French authorities were to impose a minimum capital requirement of 8 million ECU for French banks and the UK authorities were content to require the minimum capital fixed by the directive (that is, 5 million ECU), the French authorities could not seek to oppose the setting up, or the carrying on of the activities in France, of branches of UK banks, notwithstanding the fact that the level of their capital funds (in their home country, that is the UK) was inferior to that which French law requires for French banks.

There is, therefore, a risk that the authorities of one Member State by providing for a stricter regime than that envisaged by the Second Banking Directive will, in fact, be placing their own banks at a competitive disadvantage in relation to those banks of other Member States operating in their territory by means of a branch (or by virtue of the freedom to provide services).

This same risk of reverse discrimination will be present, for

11. Proposal for a Council Directive on a solvency ratio for credit institutions, COM (88) 194 final: OJ (1988) C135/4, 25 May 1988.
12. Proposal for a Council Directive on the own funds of credit institutions, COM (88) 15 final: OJ (1988) C32/2, 5 February 1988.
13. Commission Recommendation on large risk exposure (87/62/EEC), OJ L33/10, 4 February 1987.
14. Commission Recommendation on deposit guarantee schemes (87/63/EEC), OJ L33/16, 4 February 1987.

example, if the authorities of one Member State seek to impose more exacting requirements than those provided for in the said directive with regard to the maximum percentage allowed (concerning the banks' own funds) of any participation in industrial or commercial undertakings which the bank may hold. If, instead of applying the maximum authorised percentage in terms of the Second Banking Directive, the authorities – for example, the UK – establish a lower maximum level, indeed a zero level, such authorities would place their own banks at a disadvantage *vis-à-vis* (for example) German banks operating in the UK by way of branches or by virtue of the freedom to provide services (always assuming that the German authorities retain the maximum authorised percentage as laid down in the Second Banking Directive).

It should be noted in this respect that according to several decisions of the court, this possibility of reverse discrimination, notwithstanding the distortions of competition which it might involve for national undertakings, is not contrary to Community law.[15] It has been suggested by some experts that the risk of reverse discrimination, which is allowed by the provisions of the Second Banking Directive, could be declared by the Court of Justice to be contrary to the Treaty on the basis of art. 3(f) which imposes on Member States the obligation to institute 'a system ensuring that competition in the common market is not distorted'.[16] It is submitted that the court is unlikely to uphold that argument.

On the basis of these decisions, it is likely that any national supervisory authorities who seek to impose more exacting requirements on their undertakings than those minimum levels provided for in the Second Banking Directive, will come under increasing pressure from such national undertakings to align their regulatory systems to those of such Member States' authorities who simply apply the minimum levels fixed by the directive.

An additional difficulty in this respect may arise from the fact that some countries presently forbid some of their financial

15. See Opinion of Advocate-General Rozes in *Procureur de la République and Comité National de Défense contre l'Alcoolisme* v *Alex Waterkeyn and others; Procureur de la République* v *Jean Cayard and others*, Case 314–316/82, 14 December 1982, [1982] ECR 4337; *Driancourt* (Public Prosecutor) v *Cognet-Centre Leclerc*, Case 355/85, [1986] ECR 3231; *Nederlandse Bakkerij Stichting and others* v *Edah BV*, joined cases 80 and 159/85, 13 November 1986, [1986] ECR 3359 and *Ministère Public* v *A Mathot*, Case 98/86, 18 February 1987.

16. See J. Pardon, President of the Legal Committee of the European Banking Federation, in the transcript of a conference held in April 1988 at the Institut Français des Relations Internationales on 'L'intégration Financière', at p. 23.

institutions from operating outside the national borders. EEC law does not require these restrictions to be removed, but they may not be relied upon to keep out foreign institutions seeking to set up a branch or to exercise the freedom to provide services on the local market.[17]

Developments concerning banks operating retail banking in other Member States

The removal of restrictions to capital movements

Given the limitations of space, a detailed analysis of the directive of 24 June 1988 will not be provided here. Instead, two observations only will be made.

(a) *First observation: the reservation of the right of Member States to subject capital transfers to certain conditions.* Under the exception of certain transitional provisions, the directive must be incorporated in the legal systems of the Member States by means of national implementing legislation by 1 July 1990 at the latest.

However, it would be quite unrealistic to assume that from that actual date individuals established in a Member State, where there were in force certain exchange control restrictions, could immediately transfer their savings to another Member State without any control whatsoever.

Both the directive (art. 4) and the decisions of the court relative to art. 67 of the Treaty[18] reserve, in fact, a right to Member States:

> 'to take all requisite measures to prevent infringements of their laws and regulations, *inter alia* in the field of *taxation* and prudential supervision of financial institutions, or to lay down procedures for the declaration of capital movements for the purposes of administrative or statistical information'.

This right, however, is subject to the provision that 'the application of those measures and procedures may not have the effect of impeding capital movements carried out in accordance with Community law'.[19]

17. It has been suggested, however, that the Second Banking Directive, once in force, would create an absolute right for local credit institutions to exercise their activities in other Member States, with the proviso, however, that individual Member States may then seek to obtain a derogation from the directive allowing them to continue to keep in force provisions of national law forbidding certain local credit institutions from carrying out (some of their) activities abroad.
18. See footnote 6.
19. See art. 4 of the directive of 24 June 1988, footnote 1.

The exchange control systems (or two-tiered exchange rate systems) presently in force in certain Member States are implemented, not only for monetary purposes, but also for fiscal reasons. The information supplied by individuals which seek to transfer or keep financial assets abroad, or to acquire assets in another Member State, is transmitted whether systematically or in response to a specific request, to the national fiscal authorities. This is in order that such authorities may ensure that the income generated from such assets held abroad will, in fact, be declared by the individuals concerned in their tax declarations. The same holds true for SMEs.

Therefore, the removal of exchange controls in such circumstances could deprive the national fiscal authorities of an extremely important source of information.

This is the reason why the French authorities are, at this very moment, reportedly considering legislation which would be introduced simultaneously with the removal of exchange controls. This legislation would oblige their residents to make capital transfers abroad via the intermediary of a bank established in France, which bank would, without doubt, keep the fiscal authorities informed (whether systematically or in response to a direct request) of any such transfers so effected.[20]

These procedures, as far as they impose an obligation to declare transfers only and do not make such transfers subject to authorisation, appear to be compatible with the jurisprudence of the court provided that they apply only to transfers over a certain significant level.[21]

However, the question of the compatibility with Community law of the Danish legislation recently enacted in this field is more

20. See the statement made by M. Marc-Antoine Autheman, Senior Administrator of the French Treasury while speaking at a seminar organised by the French Banking Federation on 16 March 1988 on the subject, '1992: Quel Droit Bancaire?' (1992: What role for banks?) *Revue Banque*, Paris, 16 March 1988 at p. 183: 'We desire to be able to continue to insist that in certain circumstances, if not indeed, across the board, transfers destined for abroad must be effected through a financial intermediary (established in France)' [own translation].

21. See footnote 6, notably at Ground no. 35. See also the recent judgment of the Court of Justice of 14 July 1988 in *Ministère Public* v *Lambert, René*, Case 308/86, OJ (1988) C215/11, 17 August 1988: 'As Community law now stands, rules which require exporters to have foreign currency payable in respect of their sales paid through a bank and which prohibit them taking payment in bank notes, are not a barrier to the liberalisation of payments connected with trade in goods which is incompatible with Article 106 of the EEC Treaty.' Indeed, payment in cash of export sales is not a normal way of settlement of such sales (as opposed to say the payment in cash of hotel bills abroad).

complex. According to the 'statements relative to the directive of 24 June 1988' made by the Council and the Commission, the Danish authorities had reserved the right to introduce – and have since introduced – into their national legislation, provisions in terms of which a Danish resident seeking to open a personal account abroad (that is, an account which is not intended to service commercial transactions there) will be required:

(i) to request that the foreign bank undertakes to supply to the Danish authorities, the same annual information relating to interest and capital which the Danish banks themselves must furnish: and
(ii) to provide a power of attorney to the Inland Revenue Directorate to examine the account in the banking institutions.

In the same way, if the Danish resident wishes to register foreign securities directly with a financial institution situated abroad, he will be required to request that foreign financial institution to undertake to supply the necessary information to the Danish fiscal authorities. In both cases, if the banking institution abroad does not submit the report to the Danish tax authorities, these authorities may require the Danish resident to terminate the account abroad.

The German and Luxembourg delegations have observed at the time of the enactment of the 24 June 1988 directive that 'the contemplated [Danish] measures do not amount to a Community law enactment and do not create any obligation whatsoever [for the other Member States] to proceed with an automatic exchange of information relating to investment income'.

For its part, the Commission has emphasised that the measures contemplated at the time by the Danish authorities:

(a) could not be contrary to the laws in force in the other Member States concerned;
(b) could not impose any direct obligation on foreign banks *vis-à-vis* the Danish authorities; and
(c) could not affect the validity of the contractual relations between the foreign financial institution and its client.

It is presumably in order to attempt to meet these objections that the Danish measures, as enacted by way of Decree of 31 August 1988, provide, in addition, the following (s. 9(5)):

Residents unable to obtain the declaration (required from the

> foreign bank by the Danish tax authorities) may be granted exemption by Danmarks National Bank if the resident is able to document a particular need for the account to be held [and if the] Danmarks National Bank has knowledge that banking institutions in the country concerned do not wish, or according to the [foreign] country's legislation are not allowed, to assume such a reporting obligation. In such case, the resident shall file a declaration by which the resident enters into the obligation to submit documentation of the crediting of interest and account balances, together with the annual income tax return, to the tax authorities.

It is submitted that the fact that the granting of the exemption is at the complete discretion of the Danish authorities, and the fact that the exemption only relates to the holding of an account abroad, to the exclusion of the safekeeping of securities with a foreign bank, may give rise to a challenge before the Court of Justice (as a result of a reference for a preliminary ruling by a national Danish Court) on the ground that they place, at least in some instances, excessive restrictions on the rights granted to Danish residents by the Treaty and the directive of 24 June 1988.[22,23]

(b) *Second observation: directive not conditional upon prior harmonisation of various national fiscal regimes.* The directive provides (art. 6, para. 5) that the Council must take a position on the proposals to be submitted by the Commission no later than

22. It will be remembered that in the case of *Luisi and Carbone* referred to in footnote 6, the Court of Justice took the view that the applicable Italian foreign exchange regulation, prohibiting the export of foreign currency in excess of a certain amount for the purposes of business or tourist travel, was an excessive restriction on the right granted to Italian residents under the Treaty (namely the right to 'buy' hotel and restaurant services in other EEC countries) notwithstanding the fact that the Italian authorities could, in their discretion, grant an exemption (at least for business travel) to allow the export of a higher amount of foreign currency than that normally allowed.
23. It will be remembered that the Commission has taken the view in the past that the safekeeping of securities by a bank is a banking service, the restriction of which by anti-competitive agreement is forbidden by art. 85 of the Treaty. See the decision of the Commission in *Re Association Belge des Banques* of 11 December 1986, (13/87), OJ L7-27, 9 January 1987, and the reference made therein to the initial communication of objections of the Commission. See further, Marc Dassesse, 'EEC competition law affecting banking: recent developments and future prospects', *Journal of International Banking Law*, 1988, p. 105 seq., especially at p. 113. Query whether the aforementioned Danish legislation is not an excessive restraint on the right of Danish residents to 'buy' safekeeping services provided by foreign banks established in other EEC countries?

30 June 1989. These proposals are to be put forward with the aim of eliminating or reducing risks of distortion of competition, tax evasion and tax avoidance linked to the diversity of national systems for the taxation of savings and for controlling the application of these systems. The directive recalls in this regard that 'any tax provisions of a Community nature shall, in accordance with the Treaty, be adopted unanimously'. Indeed, the qualified majority voting rule introduced by the Single Act does not extend to fiscal matters.

It is important to underline, however, that if, as seems likely, the Council is not in a position to reach agreement on measures of fiscal harmonisation within the prescribed period, this delay will not affect the entry into force of the directive as scheduled.

This point is significant: it will be seen, in fact, in a later section of this chapter that it is likely that the distribution of retail financial services (especially investment products), in particular by way of the freedom to provide services, will develop in direct consequence to the systematic exploitation of the competitive distortions and divergences existing between the differing national fiscal systems of the Member States.

The single banking licence and the agreed list of banking activities

Chapter 3 examines in detail the provisions of the Second Banking Directive concerning the above topic. Accordingly, only a brief summary of the principles involved in the Second Banking Directive will follow here.

Provision of services

As a general rule, any bank validly established in one Member State may provide its services in another Member State, without being established there, providing:

(i) that it notifies its intention to the supervisory authorities of its own country (the home country);
(ii) that the services it proposes to provide are those included in the list of qualifying activities contained in the annex to the said directive; and
(iii) that the bank is so authorised to provide such services in its own country (even if the local banks of the host country are not so empowered).

The regime provided for in the said directive includes within its scope, under certain conditions, non-banking institutions controlled and guaranteed by banks which perform the activities listed in the said annex thereto and for which activities, the banks themselves, in certain Member States, are not so authorised to perform directly.

Freedom of establishment

As a general rule, any bank validly established in one Member State may set up a branch in any other Member State (host country), having only to comply with the regulations in force in its own country (home country). In addition, such a branch so set up may provide any of those services included in the qualifying list of activities contained in the annex to the said directive, provided that the bank itself is so authorised to perform such activities in its own country (this applies even where the local banks are not so empowered).

To make reference to the terms of the Second Banking Directive itself, the list of agreed banking activities 'has been drawn up on a liberal universal banking model'. The most important and far-reaching aspect of the list is the inclusion of all forms of transactions in securities. A simplified procedure is, in addition, provided for in order that the list may be periodically updated to include new services developed by the market, without there being any need to amend the said directive itself.

The principle of mutual recognition of national financial techniques

This issue is, without doubt, one of the most sensitive raised by the Second Banking Directive. It is of particular significance in the area of retail banking.

Competences of Member States to prohibit or restrict 'in the interest of the public good'

According to the recitals of the said directive 'Member States should ensure that there are no obstacles to the activities benefiting from mutual recognition being undertaken *using the financial techniques of the home Member State*, as long as the latter are not in violation of the legal provisions governing the public good in the host Member State'.

Even though the articles of the directive dealing with the right of establishment and the freedom to provide services (arts. 16, 17 and 18) do not reiterate the requirement of mutual recognition of the financial techniques of the home Member State by the host Member State, it is submitted that the reference made to this requirement in the preamble of the directive must be taken into account in order to determine the scope of the relevant articles of the directive.

It seems, therefore, that the directive makes a distinction between those activities included in the list and those not so included, not only as far as the right to exercise the activity itself is concerned, but also as regards the method of its exercise.

This consideration seems to have been taken account of in the actual provisions of the said directive in the following way:

(a) *Activities not included in the list*: the host country retains the right to prohibit the exercise of such activities by the foreign bank 'in the interest of the public good' even if the foreign bank is validly authorised to exercise such activities in the home country.[24] It should be stressed, however, that the discretion that the host country retains in respect of activities not included in the list remains, as always, subject to the limitations imposed by the general rules of the Treaty (such as (i) prohibition of discrimination on grounds of nationality or place of residence and (ii) prohibition of restrictions which are disproportionate to the purpose they seek to achieve) and, in that respect, subject to the control of the Court of Justice.

(b) *Activities included in the list*: the authorities of the host country cannot seek to prohibit the exercise of such activities in as much as the said activities are authorised by the competent authorities of the home country of the foreign bank, and this applies equally where the local banks are not allowed to perform such activities (reasoning, *a contrario*, from art. 17.4 and 17.6).

Host country control over qualifying activities

Nature of the controversy There is general agreement among the relevant commentators that the Second Banking Directive removes the discretion of the host country to invoke 'the interest of the public good' in order to prevent a bank from another Member State from exercising any of the qualifying activities where it is

24. See art. 17.4 and 17.6 of the proposal for the Second Banking Directive cited at footnote 2: 'The competent authorities of the host Member State . . . may decide, in the interest of the public good, to prohibit the credit institution from engaging in some of the activities envisaged, where the conditions of authorisation in its home country do not preclude such activities, *but those activities are not contained on the list in the annex*'.

so authorised in this respect in its home country. However, it is rather considerably less clear to what extent the authorities of the host country retain competence to require that such activities are carried out in conformity with the host country's own national legislation.

Position adopted by the Economic and Social Committee According to the Opinion of the Economic and Social Committee adopted in September 1988, the authorities of the host country would retain the right to require compliance by a foreign bank with all national legislation of an overriding, binding nature, that is those mandatory rules which the parties may not contract out of, and which legislation is aimed to prevent distortions of competition or to promote consumer protection.[25]

Therefore, in terms of the said Opinion of the Economic and Social Committee, the authorities of the host country would be able to insist on compliance with all the local legal provisions relating to price advertising and, more generally, the transparency of the conditions of sale or of providing the service, the regulation of sales or provision of services tied to premiums etc., the regulation of misleading advertising; the prohibition on the illegal trading or soliciting of certain securities etc.[26]

The competent authorities of the host country would equally retain the power, in terms of the above Opinion, to require compliance with:

> the relevant legal provisions of contract law which bind the contracting parties with a view to protecting the interests of the weaker, or less well informed party. While it is true that these (provisions) may amount to an obstacle to the freedom to provide services, the relevant interests in question, however, require that these substantive national legal provisions of the Member States designed to ensure binding protection for the (parties abovementioned) remain in force.[27]

In terms of the above, the ESC is of the opinion, 'that the only solution would be to implement in all the Member States, and at the latest by the entry into force of the second [banking] directive, the provisions of the Convention on the law applicable to contractual obligations, signed by the Member States at Rome on 19

25. Opinion of the Economic and Social Committee, ESC 287/88/final EC at para. 1.6.3.3.
26. See footnote 25 at paras 1.6.3.1 and 1.6.3.2.
27. See footnote 25 at para. 1.6.4.3.

June 1980'. These provisions aim, notably, to ensure that the consumer is not denied the protection of those mandatory legal rules applicable in that state where he has his habitual residence.[28] In this regard, the customer can only be summoned before a court having the requisite jurisdiction by reason of the customer's residence.[29]

Certain writers[30] have not failed to point out, in support of this opinion, that art. 44 of Council Directive 85/611/EEC of 20 December 1985 on the co-ordination of laws, regulations and administrative provisions relating to undertakings for collective investment in transferable securities[31] expressly provides that 'A UCITS which markets its units in another Member State must comply with the laws, regulations and administrative provisions in force in that State which do not fall within the field governed by this Directive' and in particular: 'Any UCITS [which advertises] its units in the Member State in which they are marketed must comply [with] the provisions governing advertising in that State'.

If this was indeed the import of the Second Banking Directive, it is submitted that the said directive would mark only a limited advance for the liberalisation of the provision of financial services, particularly in the area of retail banking, throughout the Community.

Indeed, generally speaking, all national provisions which, in a given Member State, are designed to ensure fairness in commercial dealings and protection for the consumer etc. are always in the nature of mandatory rules which cannot be contracted out of by the parties and which the national courts must apply even where the contract is expressed to be governed by the law of another Member State.

Consequently, the approach outlined by the ESC in its Opinion means that, in practice, banks established in one Member State which seek to provide their services to individuals or SMEs etablished in another Member State, will have to ensure that their services comply, *in all respects*, with the applicable local legislation.

28. See art. 5 of the Convention on the law applicable to contractual obligations (the Rome Convention) of 19 June 1980. See further the report of Agence Europe of 22 December 1988, No. 4920, p. 13 regarding the signature by representatives of the Member States of two protocols authorising the Court of Justice to interpret the Rome Convention (which is not yet in force).
29. See art. 13 of the Convention between the Member States on the jurisdiction and enforcement of judgments in civil and commercial matters signed at Brussels on 16 September 1968.
30. See J. Pardon, footnote 16. See also the transcript of the speech of Mr Pardon at the seminar referred to in footnote 20.
31. UCITS, OJ (1985) L375/3, 31 December 1985.

The cost of such a policy, of course, will render the freedom to exercise such activities illusory, particularly with regard to the provision of cross-border services.

It will be seen, on the other hand, that the distinction between provisions designed to ensure bank solvency on the one part, and provisions designed to regulate monetary policy on the other, is not always an easy one to make. For example: in France, national legislation prohibits banks from making interest payments in respect of credit balances held in current account. Assuming that the directive was already in force, could a foreign bank operating by way of a branch in France (and not subject to a similar regulation in its home country) pay interest to the customers of its French branch in respect of the credit balances in current account? The answer will, it is suggested, be in the affirmative if the provision is viewed, as a matter of EEC law (thus subject to review by the Court of Justice), as a measure designed to ensure the solvency of financial institutions. Indeed, in that case, the authorities of the host country, i.e. France, have no competence over French branches of banks established in other Member States. On the other hand, the answer will presumably be in the negative if the French legal provision is viewed, again as a matter of EEC law, to be a monetary policy measure for which the authorities of the host Member State retain regulatory powers.[32]

The distinction between measures designed to afford protection to the consumer on the one part and measures designed to ensure the solvency of financial institutions on the other part is also sometimes difficult. Thus, for example, in certain Member States (for example, Italy) legal provisions prohibit banks conducting mortgage credit business from extending loans in excess of a certain percentage of the value of the relevant property. However, in other Member States (for example, the UK) there are no such restrictions.[33] Assuming that the Second Banking Directive was already in force, could a UK bank extend mortgage facilities of up to 100% of the value of a building in Italy? The reply to this question would appear to depend on whether the relevant Italian regulation is considered – as a matter of EEC law – to be (i) a means to ensure the solvency of Italian banks by preventing the granting of insufficiently guaranteed credit, or (ii) a means to protect borrowers from falling into excessive debt, or (iii) a means to limit, for monetary reasons, the volume of mortgage credit extended.

32. Note in this respect, the decision of the Court of Justice of 21 September 1988 in *P. Van Eycke* v *ASPA S.A.*, Case 267/86, as yet unpublished in the ECR.
33. Cf: *The Economist* of 24 September 1988, at p. 114.

Solution to the controversy? Guidance from the decisions of the Court of Justice The above analysis is, in fact, based on the assumption that for as long as there remains an absence of harmonisation (a somewhat fanciful objective) of *all* mandatory legal provisions of the various Member States in the area of fairness of commercial dealings, protection of the consumer etc., the Member States, themselves, will retain exclusive and unlimited sovereignty to determine which provisions, according to their national legislation, amount to mandatory rules justified 'in the interest of the public good' in the sense of the term as it appears in the Second Banking Directive.

It is submitted that the above analysis is not, however, in accordance with the general principles of Community law, to the extent that such principles may be extrapolated from the jurisprudence of the Court of Justice.

According to the Court, any recourse to the provisions or principles of any national law, in order to interpret the scope of a term contained in a Community directive must be made with the unity and effectiveness of Community law in mind.[34] Any such interpretation must therefore be made under the eventual supervision of the Court of Justice which thereby ensures that Community law is interpreted and applied on a uniform basis.

In order to determine whether a national legal provision amounts to a mandatory rule justified 'in the interest of the public good' (fairness in commercial dealings; protection of the consumer, etc.,) as the term is used in the Second Banking Directive, it is necessary, or it will be necessary, to have regard to the notion of the 'public good' not as it is variously defined in the different Member States, but, rather, as it will be defined by the Court of Justice, in order to ensure a uniform application of the directive.

Role reserved to the national courts and to the Court of Justice The Second Banking Dirctive expressly provides for a right of appeal in the host country against 'any measure . . . involving penalties or restrictions on the provision of services [or on the freedom of establishment]'. The existence of such a right of appeal will enable the undertaking concerned thereby to request that the local court having jurisdiction makes a reference for a preliminary ruling to

34. See *Molkerei-Zentrale, Westfalen Lippe GmbH, Firma* v *Hauptzollamt Paderborn*, Case 28/67, 3 April 1968, [1968] ECR 143; *Walt Wilhelm and others* v *Bundeskartellamt*, Case 14/68, 13 February 1969, [1969] ECR 1; *Internationale Handelsgesellschaft mbH* v *Einfuhr- und Vorratsstelle für Getreide und Futtermittel*, Case 11/70, 17 December 1970, [1970] ECR 1125.

the Court of Justice in order to establish the compatibility (or not) of the restrictions invoked by the host country 'in the interest of the public good' with the said directive.

It is likely, in light of the recent decisions of the Court of Justice in the area of the provision of services and the freedom of establishment for insurance companies,[35] that the court will interpret this 'public order/general public interest' ground, in a much more restrictive manner than that suggested by the ESC. In fact:

(a) It can be inferred from the insurance decisions that the host country cannot invoke national provisions, designed to ensure consumer protection, to restrict the provision of financial services directed at commercial undertakings which have no need of such specific protection.
(b) It can be seen from earlier decisions of the Court of Justice that art. 36 of the Treaty, which expressly allows the Member States to introduce restrictions to the free movement of goods and, by analogy, the free movement of services[36] on the grounds *inter alia* of consumer protection, does not, however, give Member States the right to insist on absolute compliance by undertakings established in other Member States with such national consumer protection legislation. In order that such national provisions may be deemed to fall within a justified restriction to the freedom to provide services (or the free movement of goods) in the Community, such national provisions must be reasonable and proportionate to the result to be achieved:

> (such measures) are justified only if it is established that they are necessary in order to attain the objective of protection referred to in art. 36 and that such protection cannot be achieved by means which place less of a

35. See judgment of the ECJ, 4 December 1986 in *Commission* v *France*, Case 220/83; *Commission* v *Denmark*, Case 252/83; *Commission* v *Germany*, Case 205/84; *Commission* v *Ireland*, Case 206/84, [1986] ECR 3663; 3713; 3755; and 3817, respectively.
36. See *Coditel* v *Ciné Vog*, Case 62/79, [1980] ECR 881; also *Cinéthèque S.A. and others* v *Fédération nationale des cinémas français,* joined Cases 60 and 61/84, [1985] ECR 2605, and the opinion of Advocate-General Sir Gordon Slynn.

restriction on the free movement of goods within the Community.[37]

(c) In addition, the Court of Justice declared some years ago that art. 36 cannot be construed as extending to the protection of the economic or fiscal interests of the Member State.[38] It has recently adopted the same position in respect of art. 56 of the Treaty, under which national provisions providing for special treatment for foreign nationals may escape being subject to art. 59 (which prohibits restrictions on the free provision of services) if they are justified on grounds of public policy.[39]

It can, therefore, be concluded, in the light of the above jurisprudence of the Court of Justice, that if the Second Banking Directive is adopted in its present form, we shall see, in the course of the next few years, numerous references for a preliminary ruling being made to the Court of Justice. These references will be made in order to define exactly the compatibility with the general principles of the Treaty and with the provisions of the Second Banking Directive, of the numerous national provisions which will doubtless be invoked by individual Member States on the ground of the public good to oppose the marketing in their territory of financial services or financial products[40] which conform to the

37. See *Commission* v *Belgium*, Case 155/82, 2 March 1983, [1983] ECR 531 at p. 543, Ground 12. See also the following decisions: *Procureur du Roi* v *Benoît and Gustave Dassonville*, Case 8/74, 11 July 1974, [1974] ECR 837; *Enka BV* v *Inspecteur des Invoerrechten en Accijnzen, Arnhem*, Case 38/77, 23 November 1977, [1977] ECR 2203; *Frans-Nederlandse Maatschappij voor Biologische Produkten BV*, Case 272/80, 17 December 1981, [1981] ECR 3277; *Industrie Diensten Groep BV* v *J. A. Beele Handelmaatschappij BV*, Case 6/81, 2 March 1982, [1982] ECR 707; *Oosthoek's Uitgeversmaatschappij BV*, Case 286/81, 15 December 1982, [1982] ECR 4575; *Commission* v *Germany*, Case 247/81, 28 February 1984, [1984] ECR 1111; *Yaourt Surgelé*, Case 298/87, 14 July 1988; *Commission* v *Germany (Beer)*, Case 178/84, 12 March 1987; and *BLE-DUR*, Case 407/85, 14 July 1988; the latter three cases are as yet unpublished in the ECR.

38. See *Commission* v *Italy*, Case 95/81, 9 June 1982, [1982] ECR 2187.

39. See *Vereniging Bond van Adverteerders* v *State of the Netherlands*, Case 352/85, 26 April 1988.

40. Although the Court of Justice has held in *P. Van Eycke* v *ASPA S.A.* Case 267/86 (referred to in footnote 32) that for the purposes of art. 95 of the Treaty (at least) certain types of financial services, namely the opening of a savings book with a bank, cannot be assimilated to a product, it is submitted that a distinction must sometimes be made between the financial service provided by a financial intermediary of the one part, and the financial product which is the subject matter of the service provided of the other part. Thus, if a bank sells bearer bonds issued by another financial institution, the service provided by the bank in selling the bonds must be distinguished, it is submitted, from the financial product which it is selling.

regulation and financial techniques in force in the home Member State but not (in all respects) to those in force in the host Member. It is submitted that the court will hold that, in general, the following types of measures will *not* fall within the category of justified restrictions:

(a) Local consumer protection provisions imposed on a foreign undertaking operating by means of the freedom to provide services, without taking into account the equivalent measures, perhaps even more strict, to which the undertaking is subject in its own country.

(b) Consumer protection provisions invoked against those institutions providing their services to industrial or commercial undertakings or, even to individuals acting in a professional capacity.

(c) Measures which, as far as the extension of credit or granting of loans is concerned, make it compulsory to charge a minimum interest rate. These measures are normally justified by the supervisory authorities concern to ensure the solvency of the financial institutions involved. But, as has been noted, the Second Banking Directive provides that, in future, such responsibility will lie exclusively with the authorities of the home country.

(d) Measures which, as far as deposits are concerned, impose a maximum rate of deposit interest. These measures cannot be justified on the ground of consumer protection. Moreover, as has been noted, neither art. 36 (if applied by analogy to the field of services), nor for that matter art. 59, permit a Member State to enact restrictions required for the protection of their national currency. In these latter circumstances, the proper course of action for the Member State concerned is to follow the procedures laid down in the Treaty, and in the directive of 24 June 1988, concerning the taking of co-ordinated Community action in the event of monetary difficulties.

Parallel between the Second Banking Directive and the proposed Directive on Investment Services The draft which was recently prepared by the Commission concerning the proposal for a directive 'on the provision of investment services in the securities field'[41] is closely tailored to the provision of the draft Second Banking Directive.

41. See footnote 3.

The proposed Investment Services Directive which will appply to banks when providing those investment services included in the list annexed to the Second Banking Directive which are also listed in the list annexed to the proposed investment services directive, provides in particular the following:

(a) The competent authorities of the home Member State shall have exclusive regulatory competence with regard to the licensing of Community investment firms (including 'sufficient provision against market risk in accordance with rules to be prescribed by a further co-ordinating Directive')[42], and this 'irrespective of whether or not the Community investment firm establishes a branch or provides services in another Member State'[43].

(b) Member States shall draw up prudential rules to be observed . . . by Community investment firms authorized by their competent authorities. Supervision of such prudential rules shall be within the exclusive competence of the home Member State authorities irrespective of whether or not the Community investment firm establishes a branch or provides services in another Member State'[44] and such rules shall include *inter alia* rules that are aimed at protecting the investors' interest such as (i) segregation of money and securities belonging to investors from money and securities belonging to the firm, (ii) membership of a general compensation scheme or individual arrangements which provide investors with equivalent protection[45], and (iii) rules ensuring 'so far as possible' that conflicts of interest do not arise between the firm and its clients. It is further provided in that respect that the rules referred to in (i) and (ii) may be waived by individual Member States when the services are provided to business or professional investors.

42. See footnote 3 at art. 8.1.
43. See footnote 3 at art. 8.2.
44. See footnote 3 at art. 9.1.
45. Pending further harmonisation of guarantee schemes, local branches of foreign investment firms are required to participate to the compensation scheme in force in the host Member State provided that payment or contribution to such a compensation scheme shall be calculated by reference to their income in respect of investment activity carried out in that Member State only. (See art. 9.1, 3rd para.) On the other hand, the guarantee scheme of the home country only will apply when the activities are exercised in the other Member State by the exercise of the freedom to provide services (that is, without having recourse to a local branch).

(c) As far as the rules governing the relationship between investment firms and their clients (conduct of business rules) are concerned, the Commission is of the opinion that they should remain, pending further harmonisation, within the competence of the host country authorities *provided* such rules are justified on the grounds of public good.[46] Express reference is made in this respect by the Commission, in the preamble of its proposal for a directive, to the criteria laid down by the Court of Justice in the German insurance case (205/84).

RELATIONSHIP OF PROVISIONS ON SERVICES AND FREEDOM OF ESTABLISHMENT

The 'theory of cumulation' holds essentially that:

> an economic operator, of whatever nature, will have the choice between two different ways to operate in another Member State of the Community: by establishing itself there; or by providing cross-border services from the head office. But it would not be able to operate by means of simultaneously exercising the two freedoms'.[47]

Numerous large banks having their head office in one Member State are already present in one or several other Member States and are operating there by means of branches. If one were to apply the above theory, it would follow that for these banks, if, for example, their head office was in Member State A, they would not be able to provide their services in Member State B, whether from their head office or from a branch set up in another Member State, if such banks already had a branch set up in Member State B.

Such an approach would act as a tremendous restraint on the new possibilities presented by the Second Banking Directive, for it is precisely by taking advantage of the differences between the services provided in the home country and those offered by the

46. See footnote 3 and p. 73–80.

47. See P. Clarotti, Head of Division, 'Banks and financial establishments', DG XV of the EC Commission, while speaking at the seminar referred to in footnote 20 at p. 140 [own translation].

local banks (host country) that the provision of services throughout the Community may develop in the banking sector.

In contrast with the opinions advanced by some writers,[48] the decision of the Court of Justice in the case 205/84, *Commission* v *Germany* (insurance case),[49] by no means legitimated the theory of cumulation and, indeed, the Commission, for its part, firmly opposes it: 'There exist two different freedoms [freedom of establishment and freedom to provide services] and therefore, any economic operator may benefit therefrom, *even simultaneously*, on the condition that it does not use the one [provision of services] to evade the regulations relating to the other [the right of establishment]'.[50]

In addition, it will be noted:

(a) that the Second Non-Life Insurance Directive which was enacted on 22 June 1988[51] expressly recognises, with regard to the so-called large risks, the right to exercise cumulatively the freedom of establishment in one Member State and the freedom to provide services in the same Member State either from the home country of the insurance company concerned, or from another branch of that insurance company established in another Member State[52]; and

(b) that the Second Banking Directive expressly provides in art. 21.2:

> Article 18 (which provides that a bank of one Member State wishing to provide services in another Member State must notify said intention to the authorities of the home Member State, which will in turn inform the authorities of the host Member State) shall not adversely affect rights acquired before the entry into force of the provisions adopted in implementation of this directive

48. See J. Biancarelli, Head of Legal Affairs of Crédit Lyonnais while speaking at the seminar referred to in footnote 20, especially at p. 78.
49. See footnote 35.
50. See P. Clarotti at footnote 47.
51. Directive No. 88/357/EEC, OJ L172/1, 4 July 1988.
52. See, in particular, *a contrario*, preamble, p. 2, 5th para: 'Whereas, in the interest of protecting policy-holders, Member States should, at the present stage in coordination, be allowed the option of limiting the simultaneous pursuit of activity by way of freedom to provide services and activity by way of establishment; whereas no such limitation can be provided for where policy-holders do not require this protection' i.e. in the case of so-called large risks as defined by the Directive.

by credit institutions operating through the supply of services.

It is our understanding that one of the reasons behind the inclusion of this provision is to dispel any suggestion that as a result of the coming into force of the directive, banks could no longer combine, as they have often done in the past, the exercise of the freedom of establishment in one Member State (by the opening of a local branch) with the exercise of the freedom to provide services (such as large corporate loans) in that same Member State from their home base.

THE PROBLEM OF FISCAL DISPARITIES

The problem of fiscal disparities[53] can be seen to operate on two different levels.

The granting of loans and credits

The freedom to provide financial services which is at the very heart of the realisation of the internal market, is likely to raise the question of the compatibility with the fundamental principles of the Treaty of certain divergences and discriminations still existing in the area of direct taxation and withholding taxes. These issues will be in all likelihood the subject of a procedure before the Court of Justice, in the not too distant future.

The jurisprudence of the court is, in effect, settled at this moment, in the sense that the Member States have retained a considerable amount of discretion in the area of direct taxation, in the absence of any harmonisation to date in this field. However, the Member States may not exercise this discretion in such a way as to restrict the operation of the fundamental freedoms guaranteed by the

53. For a more detailed examination of this problem, see Marc Dassesse, 'Tax obstacles to banking activities in the EEC' and, annexed thereto, the preliminary report of the Belgian Commission of the European League for Economic Cooperation – tax section, Butterworth, *Journal of International Banking and Financial Law*, April 1988, p. 315 seq.

Treaty:[54] freedom of establishment, free movement of goods, freedom to provide services, free movement of persons and (from the entry into force of the directive of 24 June 1988 on 1 July 1990), the free movement of capital and of current payments.[55]

Despite such decisions, there still exists in the majority of the Member States, numerous discriminatory measures which are of such a nature as to render illusory, or at least extremely difficult, the effective provision of loans or credits by banks established in one Member State to individuals or undertakings established in another Member State. Two examples will be considered below.

Example 1: withholding tax

In such a country as Belgium (and a similar situation does exist in several other Member States), any interest paid by a Belgian national or Belgian undertaking to a bank established abroad is subject to a withholding tax of 25% (except where a reduction or exemption is applicable by virtue of applicable double taxation treaties). In contrast, if the credit is granted by a bank established in Belgium (including the Belgian branch of a foreign bank), the

54. See *Commission* v *France*, Case 220/83, – Tax credit for insurance companies, judgment of 4 December 1986 (see footnote 35), where the freedom concerned was the freedom of establishment of foreign insurance companies in France. With respect to the position in the VAT sector, see *Ministère Public and Ministry of Finance* v *Venceslas Profant*, Case 249/84, (where the freedom involved was the free movement of students within the Community), judgment of 3 October 1985, [1985] ECR 3237. With respect to the free movement of workers, see *Ministère Public* v *Y. Ledoux*, Case 127/86, judgment of 6 July 1988 (OJ (1988) C211/6): 'The Sixth Council Directive of 17 May 1977 (on the harmonisation of the laws of the Member States relating to turnover taxes – Common system of value added tax: uniform basis of assessment) prevents a Member State from levying value added tax on a motor vehicle which is owned by an employer established in another Member State where value added tax has been paid and which is used by a frontier-zone worker residing in the first Member State for the performance of his duties under his contract of employment and, secondarily, for leisure purposes'. See also the reference from the Conseil d'Etat of Luxembourg of 21 June 1988 in *Re Biehl*, Case 175/88 (OJ (1988) C 199/14): 'Does Article 7 of the EEC Treaty or any other provision of Community law, in particular Article 48 of the said Treaty guaranteeing freedom of movement for workers, prohibit a Member State from providing in its tax legislation that sums deducted by way of tax from the salaries and wages of employed persons who are nationals of a Member State and resident taxpayers during part of the year, simply because they take up residence in the country to leave it during the course of the tax year, are to remain the property of the Treasury and are not to be subject to repayment?'

55. It will be recalled that under art. 106 of the Treaty, the free movement of capital and the freedom of payments are already fully liberalised (since the end of the transitional period on 1 January 1970) when they are ancillary to the effective exercise of the four other freedoms.

withholding tax does not need to be retained by the Belgian borrower.

In addition, if the individual or undertaking who has obtained credit from abroad fails to retain the withholding tax on the interest paid to the foreign bank, he is nonetheless personally liable therefor to the Belgian Treasury.

Such a system renders it practically impossible for a foreign lender to provide its services in Belgium (unless it is prepared to open a branch there, or enters into a back-to-back agreement with a Belgian bank). The following example illustrates this point.

Let us suppose that a bank makes a loan of one million ECU at 10% interest (market rate) to an individual or undertaking, and funds intself by borrowing on the inter-bank market at 9% (market rate).

Let us further suppose that the company income tax rate in Belgium is 50%.

If the one million ECU loan is made by a bank established in Belgium, its profit margin is 10,000, on which it will pay a company income tax of 5,000. It will, therefore, retain a net benefit after tax of 5,000.

If the one million ECU loan is made by a bank established in another Member State, it will be liable to pay a Belgian tax equal to the amount of the withholding tax at source, i.e. 25,000 (25% of 100,000). This tax, therefore, amounts to 250% of the pre-tax profit (10,000) realised on the transaction.

This raises the question whether a system which imposes a tax of 250% on the profit margin of a foreign lender, as opposed to a tax of 50% on the profit margin of a domestic lender, is not a prohibited restriction on the freedom to provide banking services throughout the Community and in breach of the Treaty prohibition of discrimination on grounds of nationality or of residence.

Example 2

In several Member States, the total or partial deduction from individuals' taxable professional income of interest payments (or repayments of capital) in respect of mortgage loans is conditional on the fact that the loan is arranged between a lender and a borrower of the same Member State. This kind of discrimination obviously prevents the effective exercise of the freedom to provide services in this sector by foreign mortgage operators. Indeed, the proposal for a directive on mortgage credit, itself, provides that when a Member State grants a tax relief, it cannot make the grant of the same subject to the condition that the lender be established in its territory.[56]

However, notwithstanding the above, it can also be argued that such discrimination currently constitutes an infringement of the principles of the Treaty and that the proposed directive on mortgage credit simply confirms the existing incompatibility of such a restriction with respect to Community law. This incompatibility is two-fold: first, the discrimination as between foreign and local lenders amounts to discrimination proscribed by art. 7 of the Treaty; secondly, it involves a restriction on the free movement of workers throughout the EEC. In effect, if, for example, a French worker obtained a mortgage in France and thereafter took up residence in Belgium (meanwhile, retaining the house puchased in France for his family who continued to reside there) he would lose the right in Belgium to deduct interest payments on the loan from his taxable professional income (which payments could be so deducted if he had obtained the mortgage from a Belgian lender). In a similar field (deduction of mutual insurance contributions on the condition that the organisation be established in the same Member State as the worker making the contribution), a complaint raised by a French worker taking up residence in Belgium is presently being considered by the Commission with a view to instituting proceedings before the Court of Justice.[57]

The provision of investments and savings incentives

Several Member States have instituted voluntary pension schemes which permit individuals to deduct from their taxable income, under certain conditions, sums set aside for the purchase of shares in *approved* investment funds only. The requirement that only contributions paid to an approved investment fund will be tax deductable can be justified by the wish of the authorities to ensure that the savings of the 'future pensioners' are properly managed. What is less easy to justify is the fact that very often, approval of an investment fund is conditional on that fund investing well-nigh exclusively in local shares and bonds.

The Commission has recently announced its intention to mount

56. See the proposal for a directive concerning the freedom of establishment and the freedom to provide services in the field of mortgage credit (OJ (1985) C42/4).
57. Complaint no. 72/87 of 19 January 1987 (unpublished). See also the proposal for a directive of 21 December 1979 concerning the harmonisation of income tax provisions with respect to the free movement of workers within the Community (OJ (1980) C21/6).

an offensive against these kinds of discriminatory measures, for they re-erect the barriers that the Community is seeking to remove by the abolition of exchange restrictions. It can also be stated with regard to such measures that the Court of Justice would appear to be likely, in the light of a recent decision, to condemn them if it was called upon to consider, by way of a reference for a preliminary ruling, their compatibility with Community law after the entry into force on 1 July 1990 of the directive liberalising capital movements.[58]

Lastly, it can be presumed that foreign financial intermediaries will seek to profit from the disparities existing between the various fiscal regimes of the Member States by offering more attractive financial services to customers resident in other Member States than those on offer locally. Two examples are given below.

Example 1

In the UK, capital gains realised on the sale of a zero bond are presently taxed, in principle, at the same rate as interest obtained from an interest bearing bond. In contrast, in a country like Belgium, capital gains realised by an individual are not, as a rule, subject to any tax whatsoever. The practical result of such a disparity is that even though a zero bond issued in the UK may hold no particular attraction for a UK resident, in tax terms, it is extremely attractive to a Belgian investor (for a number of reasons, the tax advantage only exists in respect of zero bonds issued abroad and so none are issued in Belgium).

In such circumstances, therefore, it can be seen that the proposals which seek to introduce throughout the Community a uniform withholding tax at source of, say, 10% on the interest paid, would not be effective to deal with the problem. Indeed, if such proposals were adopted, they would simply lead to the favouring of certain types of foreign financial instruments in terms of which interest (or dividend) income may be paid, quite legally, in such a form as to enable the investor to avoid paying any tax thereon in that Member State where he has his tax residence. This is as a result

58. See *P. Van Eycke* v *ASPA S.A.*, Case 267/86, referred to in footnote 32, where the court held, *inter alia*, that preferential tax treatment granted to interest paid in respect of savings accounts in *local currency only*, was not incompatible with the freedom to provide services on the ground that the freedom of banking services goes hand in hand, according to art. 61(2) of the Treaty, with the liberalisation of capital movements, and that movements of capital in respect of savings accounts are not required to be liberalised under *current* EEC law (that is, before the entry into force in July 1990 of the directive of 24 June 1988).

of the fact that the fiscal legislation of that latter Member State has not made provision for the existence (and taxation) of these foreign financial assets. This situation will necessarily prevail for as long as a wide-reaching harmonisation of fiscal systems has not been achieved.

Example 2

Recent efforts have been made in the UK to organise a property income certificate market (PIC). For reasons relating to the relevant UK legislation, the issuers of PICs have been careful to ensure that these instruments are producive of investment income and not rental income (by stating explicitly that the holders of the certificates have no proprietary interest whatsoever in the property itself).

Under these conditions, the PICs do not appear from a fiscal point of view, any more attractive to the individual foreign investor than ordinary shares in a real estate company.

However, if a variety of PICs were to be developed for foreign investors, the situation could be somewhat different: for example, if the PICs were formulated in such a manner as to give to the holder of the certificate, proprietary rights in the property, the result would be, in effect, that the income produced by the PICs would be taxable in the UK. However, it would not be so taxable in that Member State where the PIC holder resided if that latter Member State had concluded a double taxation Treaty with the UK reserving the right to tax income produced by such assets to that Member State where the asset was situated (that is, in this example, the UK). Given the extremely low rates of taxation in the UK as compared to certain other Member States (for example, Belgium – marginal tax rate of 82%), it can be presumed, therefore, that such certificates would be of particular interest to holders established in other Member States where high tax rates applied even though it would presumably present little attraction for investors established in the UK.

CONCLUSION

This conclusion can only be provisional in nature, given the uncertainties which remain, notably:

(a) the absence to date of any definitive text of the Second Banking Directive (and the Directive on Investment Services in the Securities Field); and
(b) the interpretation that the court will give to such directives,

particularly as regards the public order exception which may be invoked by the host country.

However, it is possible to conclude with a reasonable degree of certainty that the entry into force of the Second Banking Directive (and the Directive on Investment Services), together with the removal (from 1 July 1990) of the restrictions to capital movements still existing in some Member States, will have, *inter alia*, the following consequences:

(a) The future exercise of the freedom to provide banking and financial services would appear to concern, first and foremost, individual customers (both as regards the granting of credit and savings deposits), as well as SMEs.

Cross-border credit transactions directed at individuals are likely to develop much more quickly as the nature of the risk to the foreign lender (not being established in the same Member State as the borrower) is principally a statistical one and this may be overcome by the determination of the relevant information in that other Member State by means of credit scoring.

The position, however, is somewhat different as far as mortgage credit is concerned in that the creation and the subsequent monitoring of the guarantees are rendered more difficult without a physical on-the-spot presence on the part of the lender.

(b) With respect to the collection of savings, the directives will, in all likelihood, enable banking and financial institutions to exploit the disparities existing between the various national legislations. This will, in turn, benefit those Member States having an 'attractive' fiscal regime and a regulatory environment which is sufficiently flexible so as not to restrict the development of new financial products. The recent 'rush' of UCITS seeking registration in Luxembourg exemplifies this trend.

(c) In the legal field, the following issues will, in all likelihood, become the subject of controversy in the years to come:

(i) The determination of the limits to the principle of the 'mutal recognition of financial techniques', which the Second Banking Directive carefully omits to define.

(ii) The determination of the relevant applicable national law to the relationship between a foreign financial intermediary (particularly where the freedom to provide services is concerned) and a customer established in another Member State (particularly where an individual, not being a professional, is concerned).

In contrast with the Second Non-Life Insurance Directive, the draft Second Banking Directive makes no provision for the determination of the law applicable to a contract between a foreign financial institution and its customer established in another Member State. This can be explained, however, by the fact that the Rome Convention on the law applicable to contractual obligations specifically excludes insurance contracts from its scope.

Moreover, the Rome Convention has only been ratified by six Member States to date (whereas at least seven ratifications are required in order for it to enter into force). Further, it seems unlikely that it will have entered into force throughout the Community as a whole, by the entry into force of the Second Banking Directive.

(iii) The determination of the extent to which the competent authorities of a Member State, or, in the event of an action before the national courts, a national judge, may require that any relevant activities carried out comply with the national legislation in force (even where the parties have chosen another law) on the basis that such legislation is justified on the ground of general public interest, or public policy or consumer protection. The solution to this question is made more difficult where the foreign law normally applicable by virtue of the provisions of the contract, itself provides for a similar, if not more extensive, degree of protection than that of the local law which is sought to be applied.

It should be noted in this respect that the directive of 21 December 1986 concerning consumer credit is to enter into force on 1 January 1990. It is suggested that this first step towards harmonisation at the level of consumer protection in the financial sector involves a parallel restriction on the discretionary powers of the Member States to require, in all circumstances, compliance with their own national legislation, even where the foreign law otherwise applicable involves a degree of equivalent consumer protection.

(iv) The problem of 'reverse discrimination': in terms of the current jurisprudence of the Court of Justice, local financial institutions will find themselves at a disadvantage as compared with those foreign institutions subject to less stringent requirements in their country of origin than those applicable in the host country.

This situation is likely to encourage those institutions established in Member States having more exacting financial regulations to create subsidiaries (or to set up joint ventures with local partners) in other Member States where the financial regulations are less stringent in order that they may service their own market from this foreign subsidiary. (For example, a UK financial institution may seek to set up a subsidiary in another Member State or a joint venture with a local financial institution, in order to sell its services on the UK market by virtue of the single licence held by the foreign subsidiary.) This technique can only be used successfully however if the foreign subsidiary is authorised under its home country rules to perform the services (comprised in the annex to the directive) which the UK parent wants it to sell on the UK market.

(v) The putting into question of the legality, with respect to Community law, of a whole series of regulatory and/or fiscal provisions, which involve, directly or indirectly, a discrimination with regard to foreign institutions or their financial products.

5—1992: THE INSOLVENCY IMPLICATIONS FOR BANKS

Roy Goode

THE SPECIAL POSITION OF BANKS AS DEBTORS

Banks are not like ordinary debtors. A special importance attaches to the integrity and stability of the banking system; if people can't trust their banks, who can they trust? There has always been a perceived need for special protection for depositors, in order to instil confidence, to avoid a run on a bank and to safeguard the depositor if a calamity does occur. Depositors are treated quite unlike ordinary creditors. In some countries they are given preferential status, in others they are protected by government-backed insurance or government guarantees. The failure of even a single bank causes nervousness; and the very existence of a system of prudential regulation carries with it, in the public mind at least, an assurance that depositors will be looked after and that banks will not be allowed to fail. Indeed, there is strong pressure on central banks to ensure that failure is avoided, not least to avoid criticism that their licensing and supervision of the failed bank have been inadequate.

BANK FAILURES IN RECENT YEARS

It is therefore not surprising that both within the EEC and outside there is considerable preoccupation with the soundness of deposit-taking institutions. In Europe there were several banking failures in the early 1980s necessitating rescue operations to preserve confidence in the banking system, for example Banco Ambrosiano in Italy, Herstatt in Germany and Johnson Matthey Bank in England. In Alberta, two major banks, the Canadian Commercial Bank and the Northland Bank, collapsed in 1985 and went into liquidation, despite the infusion of funds from the Bank of Canada to the tune of nearly $2 bn; whilst in America the savings and loan associations are in a state of crisis, with deficiencies that will require the Federal Deposit Insurance Corporation to pay out to insured depositors sums which may ultimately total as much as $100 bn, an astronomical figure that has sent shockwaves throughout the United States.

If the risks confronting domestic deposit-takers can be high – an official of one of the US Federal Reserve Banks told me that the daylight exposure of a major settling bank could be as much as eight or nine times its capital – those faced by international banks are of an entirely different order of magnitude. Added to their exposures on their domestic operations are foreign exchange risk, country risk and political risk, which can generate huge losses. The volatility of the markets – which owes much to the technological ease of moving large funds from one financial centre at the close of business to another financial centre which is then opening for business – is no longer exceptional but is a fact of business life. The interdependence of the markets means that even banks situated in a country with a strong economy face vicissitudes of fortune if there is a collapse of confidence in a foreign market. The level of inter-bank indebtedness is such that the failure of a major bank in one centre is likely to have serious repercussions not only for banks in that centre but for those in other countries as well.

Yet, paradoxically, the current concern for the financial stability of banks coincides with an equally powerful move towards the so-called deregulation of financial institutions. I say 'so-called' because in my view much of what passes for deregulation is a myth. The form of control merely shifts from legislation and its application by the court to rules propounded by the designated regulatory authorities and their enforcement by administrators. Even so, certain deregulatory trends may be observed in relation to banks. In countries such as the United States which have hitherto shown a marked hostility to combining commercial banking and investment banking, the rules inhibiting such combinations are now being relaxed. In the UK, there has been a steady dismantling of the barriers confronting particular types of deposit-taking institution, of which a notable example is the increased freedom given to building societies to engage in mainstream banking business.

A further paradox is that despite the magnitude of the risks incurred by international banks in their offshore activities, the control exercised over international banks in their domestic operations is singularly lacking in relation to their overseas business.

Thus as Professor Richard Dale remarks, in his perceptive book on international banking regulation:[1]

> [b]anks operating in the United Kingdom are not subject to any reserve requirements, credit controls, interest rate ceilings or withholding taxes in respect of their Eurocurrency business, offshore banking activity being largely separated from onshore banking activity for regulatory purposes.

This lack of control is all the more serious in view of additional factors which now attract an enhanced risk of bank failure. New players have entered the field, less staid, more adventurous, more prepared to cut corners and take risks with the prospect of substantial profits. Competition has become fiercer, not only among banks themselves but between banks and other financial institutions and between financial centres. So when one bank seems to have a good idea, all the others join in so as to ensure a slice of the action, and anxieties, if any, are suppressed. Who wants to be left behind in the pursuit of the crock of gold at the end of the rainbow? Hence exposures increase, profit margins reduce, pressure mounts for deregulation. And all this happens at a time of changing attitudes by Third World countries to repayment of debt, and of a belated recognition by international banks and their governments that the avoidance of default and the deferment of write-offs through the device of refinancing cannot continue indefinitely.

Hence the EEC programme to ensure the prudential regulation of banking will be of interest in non-EEC states as well, and not merely because of access of their banks to the Common Market.

THE BASLE AGREEMENTS

A major step forward in international co-operation among supervisory authorities occurred in 1975 when the Group of Ten established the Basle Committee on Banking Regulation and Supervisory Practices. This Committee, commonly known as the Cooke Committee,[2] concluded in the same year an agreement, which became known as the Basle Concordat, laying down guidelines for the division of supervisory responsibility between home states and host states. The Concordat was revised in 1983. In July 1988 the central bank Governors of the Group of Ten endorsed the Cooke Committee's far-reaching proposals for the international

1. Richard Dale, *The Regulation of International Banking*, p. 38.
2. Its former Chairman being Peter Cooke of the Bank of England.

convergence of capital measurement and capital standards. The 1988 Basle Agreement requires a standard ratio of capital to risk-weighted assets and off-balance sheet contingent exposures. Not all assets are as risk free as cash in the bank. The riskiness of assets is fixed as a percentage of their face value, the percentage ranging from zero for cash to 100% for (*inter alia*) claims on the private sector. Off-balance sheet contingent liabilities are converted into the equivalent of an on-balance sheet direct credit liability by applying a credit conversion factor varying according to the category of liability in question. Thus, general guarantees and acceptances are given a credit conversion factor of 100% (which means that they are treated for capital adequacy purposes as if the bank were a direct borrower), whilst commitments which can be unconditionally cancelled at any time are zero-rated. This conversion factor is then multiplied by the risk weighting appropriate to the category of debtor to which the counterparty (that is, the principal debtor) belongs. Thus, if a bank issues a documentary credit on behalf of a customer whose obligations carry a 20% risk weighting and the credit is collateralised by the underlying shipment, the credit conversion factor is 50% and when this is multiplied by the risk weighting applicable to claims on the customer the resultant figure is 10% of the amount of the credit. Special rules apply to the risk weighting of foreign exchange and interest rate related contingencies. The bank's capital, as defined by the Agreement, is required to be at least 8% of the total risk value of the assets and liabilities as thus determined. For the purpose of the Agreement, capital is divided into first tier (core) capital (equity capital and published reserves) – which must represent at least half the total capital – and second tier (supplementary) capital (other reserves and, in certain conditions, hybrid debt capital instruments and subordinated term debt).

The capital adequacy requirements embodied in the Basle Agreement are concerned primarily with credit risk, not with other categories of risk. Moreover, the risk weighting, being formula based, takes no account of the strengths or weaknesses of particular borrowers from a particular institution, nor is there country differentiation except as between OECD countries and others. Accordingly it remains necessary for central banks to apply other criteria of soundness and stability.

THE EEC INITIATIVES

A plethora of EEC directives and proposed directives relevant to prudential bank regulation has descended from Brussels, much of it influenced by the Basle Agreements.

The First Banking Co-ordination Directive 1977

Under this Directive,[3] member states were required to establish a system requiring credit institutions to obtain authorisation before commencing their activities, and authorisation could not be given unless the institution had adequate separate 'own funds' and was directed by at least two reputable and experienced persons.[4] Further, pending subsequent co-ordination the competent authorities were required to establish solvency ratios of credit institutions with a view to monitoring their solvency and liquidity and the other measures which might serve to ensure that savings were protected.[5]

The 1983 Directive on the supervision of credit institutions on a consolidated basis

Under this directive,[6] a credit institution's financial situation is required to be consolidated with that of its subsidiaries for the purpose of supervision.[7]

The proposed Second Banking Co-ordination Directive

The proposed Second Banking Directive[8] contains far-reaching provisions designed (*inter alia*) to stengthen the prudential regulation of banks. Authorisation must not be given unless the initial capital is at least 5 million ECU[9] and is maintained at its starting figure;[10] shareholders or members must be identified and appraised before the credit institution is authorised;[11] a credit

3. First Council Directive of 12 December 1977 (77/780/EEC) on the co-ordination of laws, regulations and administrative provisions relating to the taking up and pursuit of the business of credit institutions (OJ L32/30 dated 17 December 1977).
4. Art. 3.
5. Art. 6
6. Council Directive.
7. Art. 3(1).
8. Proposal for a Second Council Directive on the co-ordination of laws, regulations and administrative provisions relating to the take-up and pursuit of credit institutions and amending Directive 77/780/EEC COM (87) 715 final: OJ C84/1, 31 March 1988.
9. Art. 3.
10. Art. 8.
11. Art. 4.

institution must not hold more than 10% of its own funds as a qualified participation in any one non-banking institution;[12] and the total of its qualified participations in non-banking institutions must not exceed more than 50% of its own funds.[13] Where a credit institution established in one Member State also carries on business in another Member State responsibility for supervision is divided between the home state and the host state. The home state is required to ensure the existence of sound administrative and accounting procedures and adequate internal control mechanisms,[14] and is responsible also for enforcing capital adequacy requirements, own fund requirements, solvency ratios and the general supervision of activities. The host state must take measures to require the credit institution to make provision against market risk in respect of operations on securities markets in its territory.[15] In addition, the host state retains, until further co-ordination, primary responsibility for the supervision of the liquidity of the credit institution.[16] This allocation to the host state of the liquidity aspect of solvency requirements has occasioned some surprise in British banking circles but follows the view of the Cooke Committee that the authorities of the host state 'will often be best equipped to supervise liquidity as it relates to local practices and regulations and the functioning of their domestic money markets.[17] Authorities of host and home state have a duty to co-operate.[18]

A facet of the proposed Second Directive which does not directly concern solvency requirements may nevertheless be relevant in an insolvency situation. The Second Directive introduces the concept of the single banking licence, the effect of which is that where authorisation is granted to a credit institution in one Member State that institution may set up branches or provide services in another Member State without further authorisation and irrespective of restrictions applicable to the nationals of that State.[19] The corollary, of course, is that withdrawal of authorisation by the home state requires the host state, on being so informed, to take measures to prevent the credit institution from undertaking further transactions in its territory.[20]

12. Art. 10(1).
13. Art. 10(2).
14. Art. 11.
15. Art. 12(3).
16. Art. 12(2).
17. Revised Basle Concordat, para. 2.
18. Arts. 6, 7, 12(3), 14 (amending art. 12 of the 1977 Directive), 17(3), 18(2), 19(4),(7).
19. Art. 16(1).
20. Art. 19(8).

The host state thus has no power to time the closure, or provide support, so as to minimise the loss to those who have made deposits at the branch within its territory. However, the proposed Reorganisation and Winding-Up Directive[21] will require the host state to ensure that its deposit-guarantee scheme covers such deposits.

Another anxiety caused by the concept of the single banking licence is that business will gravitate to the least regulated state, with the result that all states will be under pressure to keep or bring their controls down to the lowest common denominator permitted by the directives, with obvious implications for bank stability and solvency. Whether this fear is well founded remains to be seen. It is true that there may be an initial temptation on the part of would-be banks and bank acquirers to move to the country with the most liberal banking laws. On the other hand, when it comes to attracting deposits or other financial support, banks may find that lenders prefer to place their money in centres where the rules are stricter and the supervisory authorities more vigilant.

The proposed Directive on Investment Services

A second draft of the proposed Directive on the Provision of Investment Services in the Securities Field has recently been circulated by the Commission. This will apply to banks providing such services and will contain authorisation requirements similar to those provided under the Second Banking Directive. However, banks already authorised under that directive to carry out securities-related activities will not require fresh authorisation. It is not, however, clear why a bank conducting investment business through a subsidiary should have to go through a different regime from that applicable when it engages in the business direct.[22] The Investment Services Directive will impose requirements aimed at protecting investors' interests, as by segregation of money and securities belonging to investors from those belonging to the firm and by establishment of general compensation schemes or individual arrangements providing investors with equivalent protection.[23]

21. See p. 100.
22. The position of subsidiaries of credit institutions will be receiving further consideration.
23. Art. 8(1).

The proposed Own Funds and Solvency Ratio Directives

The EEC equivalent of the Basle Agreement is the pair of proposed directives on Own Funds[24] and Solvency Ratios.[25] Inevitably there are differences between the two proposed directives and the Basle Agreement and work will have to be done to minimise these in order to avoid difficulties between the EEC and non-EEC members of the Group of Ten.

The EC Commission has already made a recommendation on monitoring and controlling large exposures of credit institutions.[26] This was to the effect that there should be an annual reporting requirement for every large exposure of a credit institution, that is exposure to a client or group of connected clients amounting to 15% or more of the institution's own funds,[27] and that credit institutions should be prohibited from incurring an exposure to a client or group of connected clients exceeding 40% of own funds[28] or large exposures exceeding in the aggregate 80% of own funds.[29] A directive on large exposures is intended but no proposal has yet been published.

The proposed Directive on Reorganisation, Winding-up and Deposit-Guarantee Schemes

Under this proposed directive,[30] measures for reorganisation and winding-up of credit institutions are to be placed in the hands of the home state and are to be effective in other Member States, subject to consultation with those states. This is designed as an interim measure pending the conclusion of the draft European Bankruptcy Convention.[31] However, the recently revised draft Bankruptcy Convention is expressed not to apply to proceedings

24. Amended proposal for a Council Directive on the Own Funds of Credit Institutions, COM (88) 15 final (OJ no. C32, 5 February 1988, p. 2). The original proposal was made 18 September 1986 (OJ no. C243, 27 September 1986, p. 4).
25. Proposal for a Council Directive on a Solvency Ratio for Credit Institutions, COM (88) 194 final (OJ no. C135, 25 May 1988, p. 4).
26. 87/62/EEC (OJ L33, 4 February 1987, p. 10).
27. Art. 3(2).
28. Art. 4(1).
29. Art. 4(2).
30. Amended proposal for a Council Directive concerning the Reorganisation and the Winding-up of Credit Institutions and Deposit-Guarantee Schemes, COM (88) 4 final, 4 January 1988.
31. Proposed Reorganisation and Winding-up Directive, 10th recital. As to the draft Bankruptcy Convention see p. 101.

against credit institutions![32] The directive also requires Member States to ensure that the deposit-guarantee schemes existing in their territory cover the deposits of branches of institutions having their head office in another Member State.[33] The intention in due course is to produce a directive on deposit-guarantee schemes, if this proves necessary; meanwhile, there is merely a Commission Recommendation relating to such schemes.[34] Deposit-guarantee schemes exist in many countries, including the UK. Properly drawn schemes should ensure that some risk remains on the depositor, otherwise he has every incentive to bank with the institution paying the highest rates of interest, regardless of risk. The view has been expressed in the United States that deposit insurance may have some adverse effects by enabling the deposit-taking institution to continue in business long after it should have closed its doors.

The revised draft European Bankruptcy Convention

Work on an EEC Bankruptcy Convention to be concluded pursuant to art. 220 of the Treaty of Rome has now been in progress for more than 20 years, with no end in sight. The original draft Bankruptcy Convention was ultimately rejected as too complex. The Council of Europe then began work on a more modest proposal. A revised text prepared by the Committee of Experts on Bankruptcy Law of the Council of Europe[35] has recently been circulated for comment[36]. The essence of this is that where a bankruptcy is opened in a member state in conformity with the requirements of the Convention this is to constitute the main bankruptcy, and the competent authorities of other member states are expected to assist the liquidator in collecting, removing and disposing of assets within those states.[37] If bankruptcy proceedings are later opened in another member state (which may be done whether or not the debtor is insolvent in that state)[38] these secondary bankruptcy proceedings

32. Art. 1(1).
33. Art. 17(1).
34. Commission Recommendation of 22 December 1986 concerning the introduction of deposit-guarantee schemes in the Community (87/63/EEC), OJ L33 4 February 1987, p. 16.
35. Draft European Convention on Certain International Aspects of Bankruptcy (ADCDCJ8841, Strasbourg, 13 June 1988).
36. The text is as proposed in the Committee's final activity report of 15 March 1988 with amendments made by the CDCJ at its 40th meeting from 2 to 6 May 1988. An alternative version proposed by the Austrian expert has also been circulated.
37. Chapters I and II.
38. Art. 14.

will continue separately, the principle being to give protection to certain categories of local creditor – preferential and secured creditors, public law creditors and creditors whose claims arise from the debtor's operation or activities in the second state – by providing for them to be paid from local assets, only the surplus asset being transferred to the main bankruptcy to form part of the assets in that bankruptcy.[39] A creditor in a secondary bankruptcy who has received payment in that bankruptcy cannot participate in a dividend in the main bankruptcy so long as the dividend received by other creditors in the main bankruptcy is less than the dividend he received.[40]

CONCLUSION

Banks may be involved in insolvency as debtors or as creditors. The failure of a major international bank may trigger financial insecurity on the part of Community-wide recognition of authorisations granted and restrictions imposed by the competent authorities of a Member State.

The role thus thrust upon regulatory authorities by Community law sharpens the question which has already surfaced in various jurisdictions as to the extent to which the regulatory authorities themselves may incur legal liability if they grant authorisations which should not have been granted or fail to exercise proper supervision and, in consequence, depositors suffer loss.[41] The pressure will be all the greater to ensure that banks in difficulty are supported by a suitable lifeboat. One thing is certain: no amount of regulation will prevent a bank somewhere, at some time, from becoming insolvent; and with the vast volume of high-value business now able to be transacted as the result of modern technology we can be sure that when the failure of a major player occurs it is likely to dwarf anything we have hitherto experienced.

39. Arts. 18, 19.
40. Art. 21(2).
41. It has recently been held that the Bank of England owes a duty to depositors to exercise reasonable care and skill in the supervision of deposit-taking banks but owes no duty to those who are not depositors within s. 5(1)(d) of the Banking Act 1979 (now Banking Act 1987, s. 5(3)(d). For example, a parent company placing deposits with its subsidiary (*Minories Finance Ltd* v *Arthur Young; Johnson Matthey plc* v *Arthur Young, The Independent*, 20 July 1988; *The Times* 27 July 1988).

6—SECURITIES FOR INDEBTEDNESS AND THEIR REGISTRATION UNDER EUROPEAN LAW

Robert R Pennington

One of the areas of law where the laws of the European countries which are members of the European Community are most diverse, and where attempts at harmonisation will encounter most difficulty, is the law concerning the creation of security over assets of different kinds to reinforce obligations for the repayment of loans or the discharge of other indebtedness or obligations. This is admittedly no impediment to the realisation of a unified European market by 1992 in respect of transactions in and securities given over land, which by its nature can be subject to only one system of law determined by the situation of the land. Nevertheless, the diversity of Member States' laws can cause serious difficulties when the security is given over tangible moveables, particularly raw materials, semi-manufactured and manufactured goods or products which are cultivated rather than manufactured. Securities over intangible moveables, such as trade debts or loans made to third parties when the debtors are located in different countries present less of a problem, but the laws of Member States governing them are confusingly disparate.

The laws of all the Member States of the European Community in respect of securities for indebtedness are very different from those of the UK (although the Irish law resembles our own except in respect of mortgages of land). The pattern for most of the other European countries (except Germany, Denmark and Greece) has been set basically by the French Civil Code of 1804 as amended and supplemented by other legislation, and with variations of detail of the relevant law in the Benelux countries, Italy and Spain is based on the principles of French law and closely resembles it. Germany has, for historical reasons and because of judicial developments since its Civil Code came into force in 1900, a system of law governing security for obligations which is basically different from the French law, and Danish law may, without injustice, be described as being in much the same state as German law was a century ago, as may Greek law, which in the 19th century deliberately adopted the German model. In order to keep this chapter within a reasonable size, the systems of law which will be examined in some detail will be confined to French and German law, and since under both these systems the law governing securities over land is radically different from that governing securities over moveables, both tangible and intangible, this chapter will deal first with securities over land and then with securities over moveables.

SECURITIES OVER LAND AND REGISTRATION SYSTEMS

French law

The only form of security for a money obligation which may be created over land in French law is the *hypothèque*, or to give it its full name, the *hypothèque conventionelle* (contractual land charge) so as to distinguish it from the other kinds of *hypothèque* which arise automatically under French law (for example, the *hypothèque légale* which spouses have over each other's land to secure their rights to the division of property between them in accordance with their chosen matrimonial regime on the termination of the marriage); or which arise as a result of legal proceedings (for example, the *hypothèque judiciaire* which a judgment creditor has over the land of his judgment debtor to secure the judgment debt, but which can be enforced against a particular piece of land (including the buildings and accessories on it) only when the judgment has been registered against that land.)

These different kinds of *hypothèque* share a common method of enforcement, despite the difference in their origins. The *hypothèque conventionelle* is distinguished by the fact that its creation requires a valid contract between the landowner and the secured creditor (though not necessarily the borrower or debtor, if different from the landowner). For the contract to be valid it must be in the form of a notarised act, though not necessarily one executed before a notary practising in the district where the land charges registry (*bureau des hypothèques*) for the locality (*arrondissement,* or in the Seine region a sub-division of an *arrondissement*) situated in the same place as the local civil court with general jurisdiction (*tribunal de grande instance*). Registration is effected so as to preserve priority for the *hypothèque* over other interests in the same land which are later created or registered, and also so as to make the *hypothèque* capable of execution (that is, enforceable by the appropriate judicial proceedings). The amount secured by the *hypothèque* may be any money obligation, and so it may be used to secure a current account as well as a loan of a fixed amount, and the amount secured may be repayable over whatever period and on whatever terms the parties agree, including terms for the variation, respite or accumulation of interest. Moreover, the money obligation need not be that of the landowner who gives the *hypothèque*, and so a third person may charge his land to secure a debtor's personal obligation to repay a loan or other indebtedness (this is known as a *caution réelle*), and a surety for a debt may charge his land to secure his liability as a guarantor of the debtor's obligation (*hypothèque pour sûreté personnelle*).

The *hypothèque* has been described by some French authors as a security on the prospective proceeds of sale of the land charged rather than a security over the land itself, and they contrast the *hypothèque* with other proprietary interests in land owned by another person, such as servitudes and usufructs, which entitle the grantees to make use of or to take possession of the land, or to take the produce or yield from it. The distinction that a *hypothèque* charges the prospective proceeds of sale of the land and not the land itself, appears to us to be as arid as that between rents which issue out of land and periodical sums of money which are charged on land. However, it does at least have the merit of emphasising the point that the owner of a *hypothèque* can do nothing on his own initiative to obtain payment directly by using or disposing of the land which is subject to it. He cannot himself take possession of the land (as can a legal mortgagee of English land by virtue of his derivative leasehold estate), nor can he sell the land and pay himself off out of the proceeds of sale. Any provision in the notarised act creating the *hypothèque* or in a collateral contract purporting to confer any such powers on the secured creditor would be void as an attempted ouster of the court's exclusive jurisdiction over enforcement proceedings (*clause de voie parée*). *A fortiori*, a contractual provision that on the debtor failing to pay the secured debt in accordance with the contractual terms, the land charged with the debt shall become the property of the creditor (*pacte commissoire*) is totally ineffective; there is no such thing as foreclosure under French law.

The only initiative which the creditor secured by a *hypothèque* may take when the principal of the debt secured has become immediately due and payable (for example, because of the operation of a default clause in the relevant loan agreement) is to serve a notice on the owner of the land charged demanding payment within 30 days, or if he is not the debtor and the *hypothèque* is a *caution réelle*, a notice demanding payment or the relinquishment (*délaissement*) of the land for judicial sale. The notice must be registered at the land charges registry where the *hypothèque* is registered, and if the notice is not complied with, the secured creditor may apply to the court for an order that the land shall be sold by competitive bidding (*surenchère*), usually at a public auction, but not necessarily so. If the land is temporarily unsaleable or if the market is seriously depressed, the court may alternatively order that the income of the land shall be collected and retained by a person appointed by the court, but an order for sale must eventually be made before anything may be paid to the secured creditor. The court's order for the sale of the land must be published in a regional newspaper carrying legal advertisements, and other persons having claims against the prospective proceeds of sale (that is, other secured or judgment creditors) may lodge their claims within a limited time so that the court may make an order directing the application of the prospective proceeds of sale in order to discharge the *hypothèque* and the other claims according to their respective priorities. When an acceptable offer or the highest bid for the land has been made under the judicially directed sale, the court makes a final order that the accepted offeror or highest bidder shall become the owner of the land. Whereupon he may register his title under the court's order (*adjudication*) at the land charges registry, and the *hypothèque* and all other claims enforceable against the land (except *hypothèques* and other claims registered with priority to the enforced *hypothèque*) cease to exist, and are transferred to the proceeds of sale as far as it suffices to discharge those claims.

A *hypothèque* is also automatically discharged and transferred to the prospective proceeds of sale:

(a) if the owner of the land charged (not necessarily the debtor of the secured debt) is formally declared insolvent (*liquidation des biens* or *règlement judiciaire*);
(b) if execution is commenced against the land by a judgment creditor serving on the owner of the land a notice demanding payment of the judgment debt;
(c) if the court in adversary proceedings orders the land to be sold (for example, on a disputed title claim), and the insolvency order, or the notice demanding payment, or the court order directing a sale, is notified to the land charges registry.

The procedure is that the trustee in bankruptcy (*syndic*) sells the land, or the court orders its sale at the instance of the judgment creditor or in the course of the adversary proceedings, and the proceeds of sale are applied in the order directed by the court.

A creditor secured by a *hypothèque* cannot, as under English law, preserve his security intact despite the mortgagor's bankruptcy and simply prove in the bankruptcy for the excess of the secured debt over his valuation of the land. The same applies if the land is sold under an order of the court obtained by a judgment creditor of the landowner, and this is so even if the *hypothèque* was created and registered before the execution commenced or was itself registered.

One final indignity suffered by a creditor secured by a *hypothèque* on a judicial sale of the land concerned is that he can recover out of the proceeds of sale only the last three years' arrears of interest on the secured debt, even though the normal limitation period within which he may sue a debtor personally for principal and arrears of interest is 30 years.

When land subject to a *hypothèque* is sold in insolvency proceedings or under an order of the court, whether obtained by the person entitled to the *hypothèque* or not, certain unsecured creditors of the landowner may compete with the proprietor of the *hypothèque* for payment out of the proceeds of sale. They are primarily anyone who sold the land to the landowner or to any of his predecessors in title for the amount remaining unpaid of the purchase price payable on the sale, and anyone who advanced the whole or part of the purchase price to the landowner or any such predecessor in title for the amount of the advance remaining undischarged. The rights of such persons are known as *privilèges spécieux* encumbering the land, and are the equivalent of the English unpaid vendor's lien. They are both registrable in the land charges registry with priority as regards other interests in the land as from the date of registration, but if they are registered within two months after they arise, they take priority as from the date when they arise. A person who advances money to enable a purchaser of land to pay the purchase price and who takes a *hypothèque* as security is therefore well advised to ensure that the vendor is leaving no part of the purchase price outstanding, and that no one else is making a concurrent advance to provide any other part of the purchase price. Other competing claimants may be a person who has successfully taken proceedings against the landowner for the benefit of all his creditors (normally insolvency proceedings), an employee of the landowner who has a claim for unpaid remuneration, or an author, composer or artist who has a claim for unpaid royalties or other consideration for the licensing or assignment of a copyright. In so far as such creditors of the landowner cannot obtain payment out of his moveable property, they may recover the excess out of his land, and they have a *privilège général* or general charge on it which is effective against all the debtor's land without registration, and which takes priority over *hypothèques* created by him at any time.

As shown above, French law provides for the registration of *hypothèques* and various other interests in land in the land charges register of the locality, and since 1955 it also provides for the registration of transfers of the ownership of land in the same register, which has retained its original name. The French land charges register is not a register of the title to land, but instead a register of certain transactions in land, similar to our former Middlesex and Yorkshire Deeds Registries. The sanction for failing to register a registrable transaction promptly is that it cannot be enforced or relied on against another person who takes an interest in the land before or afterwards and who registers the transaction creating his interest before the first transaction is registered (*non-opposabilité*). This is subject to the exception mentioned above for the privileges of unpaid sellers, persons who advance purchase money and employers and certain other persons in respect of claims for unpaid remuneration. The result is, therefore, that *hypothèques* created on the same land, rank as between themselves in the order in which requests to register them are submitted to the appropriate land charges registry for the district in which the land is situate, and a purchaser of land takes free from *hypothèques* which have not been submitted for registration before he submits the notarial act in respect of his purchase for registration.

German law

German law recognises three kinds of security over land for obligations to pay the principal of a fixed money obligation, namely, the *Verkehrshypothek* or marketable charge, the *Sicherungshypothek* or cautionary charge, and the *Grundschuld* or abstract fixed money charge. All of these charges are created by a notarised act which is registered in the land register (*Grundbuch*), a register of title to land which is kept for each district in the country. Before it is registered the charge gives rise to no security over the land, and because German law does not recognise anything in the nature of an equitable interest in land, the charge takes effect only as a contract enforceable by the normal contractual remedies.

The difference between the *Verkehrshypothek* and the *Sicherungshypothek* on the one hand, and the *Grundschuld* on the other, is that the former can exist only if and as long as the money obligation secured by them exists, whereas a *Grundschuld* can exist even though there has never been any such obligation or even though such an obligation which did exist has been discharged. For example, a *Grundschuld* may be created to secure DM500 000 with interest at 5% per annum from a stated date, repayable on a fixed future date when neither the landowner nor the person for whose benefit the security is created has contracted to pay the principal and interest. Likewise if any such contractual obligation has been secured by a *Grundschuld*, the security does not cease to exist when the obligation has been discharged. A *Grundschuld* is therefore a completely abstract charge over land to secure a fixed amount in money. The nearest equivalent to it in English law is the charge which family settlements used to impose on settled land to secure portions for the younger children of the marriage, though the analogy is hardly apposite, since *Grundschulden* are in practice used to secure loans and debts, and not benevolences.

The *Verkehrshypothek* and the *Sicherungshypothek* are likewise securities for money, but they presuppose the existence of an obligation. The difference between them is that in the entry of a *Sicherungshypothek* in the land register the obligation it secures is identified by reference to the contract which created the secured obligation (for example, a contract of loan, or a contract for sale of the land under which part of the purchase price is left outstanding) whereas, in the entry of a *Verkehrshypothek* only the obligation itself is stated, in the same way as in the entry of a *Grundschuld*, and the parties to the contract creating the obligation are mentioned only as the applicants for registration. To ensure that the correct kind of security is registered, the entry in the register also states expressly whether it is an entry of a *Verkehrshypothek*, a *Sicherungshypothek* or a *Grundschuld*. The practical difference between a *Verkehrshypothek* and a *Sicherungshypothek* is that a person who takes a transfer of a *Verkehrshypothek* in good faith can enforce the obligation stated in the entry in the land register against the land as the entry stands, even though:

(a) it is incorrect (for example, the secured debt is stated to be DM500 000, whereas only DM100 000 has been advanced);
(b) the obligation has been wholly or partly discharged (for example, the landowner or borrower has repaid DM400 000 out of a secured loan of DM500 000 without a note of the repayment being entered on the register);
(c) the secured obligation is void or voidable (for example, for fraud or mistake) or has been altered (for example, the secured creditor has released part of the principal, or has

agreed to reduce the rate of interest or to defer the date for repayment of the principal).

This protection of the transferee of a *Verkehrshypothek* extends only to his security over the land, however. If the debt which is secured on the land is also transferred to him (which it need not necessarily be), the transferee's rights are governed by the rules governing the assignment of debts and claims, and as under English law, he obtains no greater personal rights against the debtor (whether the landowner or another person) than the original creditor had at the time of the transfer.

If a debt is secured by a *Sicherungshypothek*, the secured creditor is able to enforce his security against the land only to the same extent that the debt secured is also personally recoverable from the debtor, and if the debt is non-existent, void or voidable, or has been discharged by payment, or in any other way, the security against the land is not enforceable or, at least, its enforcement could be successfully resisted by the landowner. In other words, in this respect the *Sicherungshypothek* resembles the mortgage of land under English law, because it is accessory to and dependent on the recoverability of the debt or obligation which it secures, whereas the *Verkehrshypothek* requires there to be, or to have been, an obligation or a purported obligation which it secures, but the security it creates is independent of the obligation in that a transferee of the security in good faith may conclusively treat that obligation as being the one stated in the land register and as being valid and still existing. The *Grundschuld*, on the other hand, is wholly abstract, and both the original grantee of it and any transferee from him may enforce it against the land on which it is secured to recover the fixed amount of money specified in the land register. In practice, of course, *Grundschulden* are mostly created to secure loans and other debts, but as far as the security is concerned, that is purely coincidental.

The peculiarity of German law in notionally separating the debt secured from the security for it in the case of the *Verkehrshypothek* and the *Grundschuld* is exemplified by the fact that the security comes into existence as soon as the relevant entry is made in the land register, even though the loan or debt in respect of which it is expressed to be given has not been made or incurred, and the security continues to exist after the loan has been repaid or the debt discharged. In those circumstances the security is vested in the landowner himself, and is known as an *Eigentümerhypothek* or an *Eigentümergrundschuld* (a charge vested in the landowner), which he can transfer to a third person. If the loan or debt to be secured has not been made or incurred when the charge is registered, however, the charge becomes a *Fremdhypothek* or a *Fremdgrundschuld* (a charge vested in a third person, the lender) automatically on the loan being advanced or the debt arising. When the secured loan is discharged, other creditors who have charges on the same land which are registered after the *Verkehrshypothek* or *Grundschuld* have an interest in ensuring that the entry in respect of it in the land register is cancelled so as to prevent the landowner 'reviving' the charge by transferring it to a third person, even one who is aware of the later ranking charges. The discharge of the debt secured does not automatically discharge the *Hypothek* or *Grundschuld*. The proprietors of a second or third *Hypothek* or *Grundschuld* can require this to be done only if the landowner has so contracted, and the application for cancellation must be made by the landowner and the person entitled to the original charge jointly. Such a contractual right can be protected by the second or third chargee entering a note of his contractual right to it in the land register (*Löschungsvormerkung*), and a transferee of the redeemed first charge then has constructive notice of it and cannot maintain priority for it over the later charges.

The reason for the diversity in the forms of charges over land which German law recognises is purely historical. Before the promulgation of the German Civil Code in 1896, the standard form of security in the part of Germany on the left bank of the Rhine and in northern Germany was the *Hypothek*, modelled on the French *hypothèque*, which like the English mortgage is a purely accessory form of security. In southern Germany, on the other hand, the traditional form of security was the *Grundschuld* or *Grundpfandrecht*, which was based on traditional German (and non-Roman notions) of the pledge of land as security akin to the medieval *vadium* of English law. Nowadays, however, both the *Hypothek* and the *Grundschuld* are used throughout Germany, and the form of charge which is used for a transaction is nowadays determined by its greater suitability for the particular transaction than the other available forms.

In practice, banks and other credit institutions mostly use the *Grundschuld* to secure short- and medium-term loans or indebtedness, particularly when the amount owed is subject to variation (such as a current account) or if the rate of interest charged is variable (for example, 3% above current Lombard rate). As an alternative form of security for indebtedness which varies in amount from time to time, banks also use a form of *Sicherungshypothek* known as the *Höchstbetragssicherungshypothek* (a maximum amount cautionary charge). This is a *Sicherungshypothek* securing the amount for the time being owed to the secured creditor under a specified transaction or series of transactions (for example, the debit balance for the time being owed by a customer on an overdrawn bank account) not exceeding a fixed amount. The maximum amount includes interest and charges, and is usually fixed so as to leave a reasonable margin over the amount advanced and outstanding; such a charge is rarely transferred, but if it were, the transferee could enforce the security against the land comprised in it only to the extent of the amount which remains owing to the original secured creditor within the limit of the fixed maximum amount. Long-term loans (particularly purchase money loans) are made in Germany by specialised banks and institutions (*Hypothekenbanken* and *Bausparkassen*) which usually take *Verkehrshypotheken* to secure the repayment instalments. But *Bausparkassen* (corresponding to the British building societies) and the commercial banks which in recent years have expanded into the house purchase finance market also use *Grundschulden* as well as *Verkehrshypotheken* as the chosen form of security.

The initial proprietor of a *Hypothek* or a *Grundschuld* (that is, the secured lender or creditor) will owe his title to the security to his registration in the land register, but (except in the case of a *Sicherungshypothek*) on registering the security the land registry also issues a document to the secured creditor certifying his title to the registered security unless the entry in respect of it in the land register prohibits this from being done. The document is known as a *Hypothekenbrief* or a *Grundschuldbrief*, and it serves the same purpose as the Charge Certificate issued by the Land Registry in England and Wales in respect of a registered charge on registered land. It differs from a Charge Certificate, however, in that the security represented by it (with or without the debt secured) may be transferred by a written instrument signed by the proprietor named in the certificate or by a notarised act to which the proprietor is a party, and a title may be shown to the charge by producing an unbroken chain of such transfers to successive transferees. Normally, the transfer of such a *Briefhypothek* or *Briefgrundschuld* is effected by a notarial act, because the transfer is then equated with the entry of the transferee in the land register as the proprietor of the charge. Under the principle which protects persons who carry out transactions in reliance on the contents of the land register (dealt with below), a transferee of the charge who can produce a complete chain of notarised transfers, beginning with a transfer by the proprietor of the charge named in the land register and concluding with a transfer to himself, will be entitled to enforce the charge against the land even though the chain of transfers is defective (for example, because of fraud, mistake, incapacity or illegality), other than forgery of a notarised transfer.

There are other forms of *Hypothek* in addition to those which are transferable only by an entry on the land register (*Buchhypothek*) or which are represented by transferable certificate, but the only one which deserves particular mention here is the *Wertpapierhypothek*. This is a *Sicherungshypothek* created by a public company (*Aktiengesellschaft*) in favour of a representative of the holders of bonds of a series issued by the company or another company (for example, parent company). The bonds are invariably in bearer form, and the representative holds the security vested in him as a nominee or trustee (*Treuhänder*) for the holders of the bonds for the time being. The amount for which the *Sicherungshypothek* is registered is the principal amount of the bonds plus the total amount of interest which will become payable until the last date for their redemption plus a percentage margin as additional security. The result of this is that the amount for which the *Hypothek* is registered may well exceed the value of the land over which security is given. The bondholders can, of course, recover only the amount actually owed to them out of their security.

The law governing the enforcement of the security conferred by *Hypotheken* and *Grundschulden* is similar to the corresponding French law. Enforcement is treated by German law as a process of execution identical with the execution of a judgment for a sum of money. To avoid the need to prove that the principal amount of the secured debt is due and payable (for example, under the terms of a default clause), the proprietor of the charge always obtains from the owner of the land, on the creation of the charge, a notarised authorisation to enter judgment against him for the enforcement of the security at any time (*Vollstreckungstitel*). The court will, on production of the authorisation, order the enforcement of the charge without proof that the amount secured by it is due, unless the landowner can prove that the proprietor of the charge is acting fraudulently or otherwise improperly. The enforcement order made by the court is normally that the land and its accessories shall be sold by a public auction conducted by an officer of the court or in some other manner directed by the court. However, the court may alternatively, or initially before directing a sale, order that the income or physical yield of the land (for example, a farm harvest or the continued working of a quarry or mine) shall be received by a person appointed by the court, who may be the nominee of the secured creditor. The proceeds of sale of the land charged and the income or proceeds of the exploitation of the land must be paid into court. They are disposed of as the court directs in accordance with the respective priorities of holders of registered charges over the land, including judgment creditors who have applied to the court for the execution of their judgments and have obtained charging orders (*Zwangshypotheken*) against the land in question which they have registered in the land register. A sale of land under an order of the court is completed by the court making an order that the successful bidder at the auction ordered by the court, or the person to whom the land has been sold if it is sold otherwise than by public auction, shall be registered as the owner of the land in the land register, and he becomes the owner when this is done.

The rights of proprietors of *Hypotheken* and *Grundschulden* against the land comprised in their charges is fully preserved by German law if the landowner is adjudged bankrupt (*Konkurs*) or if he enters into a composition with his creditors which is approved by the court to avoid bankruptcy (*gerichtliche Vergleichsverfahrung*). This applies both to companies and to individual landowners. The creditors secured by charges on the land which have been registered (including judgment creditors who have obtained charging orders) may segregate the land subject to their charges from the landowner's other assets administered by the trustee in bankruptcy (*Absonderung*), and may enforce their normal remedies against the segregated land in proceedings distinct from the insolvency proceedings. The only right of the trustee in bankruptcy is to redeem the charges by paying the full amount of the loan or debt secured by them before the secured creditors obtain orders for the sale of the land. There is therefore no risk, as there is in French law, of the priority of the proprietor of a charge being adversely affected by the claims of preferential creditors.

The German registration system for land, unlike the French, involves the registration of the ownership of each parcel of land in the land register for the district, and the registration also of interests derived out of that ownership (other than leases) and of charges on it. The land register reflects the ownership of land and the presence or absence of proprietary interests and charges on it even if entries have been made in it incorrectly (for example, of dispositions which are void for illegality, fraud or incapacity), and the only remedy of the 'true' owner is to seek a court order for rectification. A person who takes a disposition of land or an interest in it in good faith and who registers that disposition is entitled to assume that the land register at the time his disposition is registered is correct and complete. The registered disposition is therefore conclusively effective against all other claimants to the land or to interests in it whose claims are not recorded in the land register (with the exception of leases) and such claimants cannot obtain rectification of the land register against the registered disponee. Dispositions include *Hypotheken* and *Grundschulden* (including *Zwangshypotheken* to enforce judgments), and consequently they rank between themselves as securities over the land in question in the order in which they are registered.

SECURITIES OVER TANGIBLE AND INTANGIBLE MOVEABLES

French law

Under French law, the basic and universal form of security for debts and money claims over tangible and intangible moveables (goods; machinery, plant and equipment not forming accessories to land; and debts, rights against third parties (*créances*), industrial property rights and investments) is the pledge (*gage*). A pledge may be given to secure any obligation to pay money or which may result in such an obligation, and so the performance of any contractual obligations may be so secured.

Pledges of tangible moveables

The form and effect of pledges differ, depending on whether they are given over tangible or intangible moveables. A pledge over tangibles or goods can be created only by agreement between the owner or presumptive owner of the goods and the pledgee accompanied by the physical delivery of the goods to the pledgee, or to a custodian for him, or to a third person who is directed to hold the goods at the pledgee's disposal. If delivery is made to such a third person, successive pledges may be created over the same goods by the owner directing him to hold the goods at the disposal of each of the successive pledgees when a pledge is created in his favour, and the pledges then rank in the order in which such directions are given. If a pledge is created by possession of the goods being delivered to the pledgee or to a custodian for him, it is, of course, impossible to create further pledges over the same goods because of the first pledgee's possession. A redelivery of pledged goods to the pledgor or to a custodian for him terminates the pledge because, as under English law, the essence of the pledgee's security is the possession of the goods.

It is impossible under French law to create a pledge over goods which the pledgor is to acquire later so that the pledge arises automatically when they come into the pledgor's possession. Such an attempted transaction creates at most a personal obligation on the pledgor to effect delivery to the pledgee when he acquires possession of the goods in the future (*promesse de gage*), and because French law does not recognise equitable proprietary interests, a pledge arises only when the goods are physically delivered to the pledgee or to his custodian. On the other hand, under French law, a pledgee is protected by the rule which applies to all persons to whom goods are delivered under sales or other dispositions if the recipient honestly believes that the person who makes delivery is the true owner of the goods or his agent. Because of their good faith, such recipients acquire a good title to the goods, and in the case of a pledge the true owner can recover the goods only by paying the pledgee the amount which is owing to him under his agreement with the pledgor.

A pledge is enforced by the court ordering the sale of the pledged goods on the application of the pledgee, and the proceeds of sale are applied as the court directs to discharge pledges on them. If the pledge is a commercial transaction, however, and the pledgee has physical control over the goods, he may sell them in order to realise his pledge without the need to obtain an order of the court.

A provision in the agreement for a pledge that the pledgee shall become the owner of the goods on the pledgor's default (*pacte commissoire*) or that the pledgee may realise his security in any other way than indicated above (*clause de voie parée*) is void.

The necessary publicity in respect of a pledge of goods is provided by the fact that, while the pledge exists, the goods are in the possession of the pledgee or a custodian nominated by him or of a third person who holds them at the pledgee's disposal, and third persons are deemed to be sufficiently warned of the existence of the pledge by that fact. Consequently, French law does not require pledges to be registered in a public or other register, except in those instances dealt with below where special legislation makes it possible to create a pledge without dispossessing the pledgor (*gage sans déplacement*).

Pledges and charges without dispossession

A pledge in the traditional form is obviously an unsatisfactory form of security for loans made to individuals or companies which carry on a business or profession, since possession of the goods will be required by the borrower either because the goods are equipment with which the business is carried on, or because the goods are raw materials which are processed or inventory or stock in trade which is disposed of in carrying on the business. Legislation has therefore made piecemeal exceptions to the requirement that a security over tangible moveables can be created only by delivery of them to the creditor.

In the first place, certain tangible moveables can have *hypothèques* created over them with the same effect as *hypothèques* over land; the rules governing such *hypothèques mobilières* are the same as for *hypothèques* over land, apart from their registration in different registers than the local land charges register. *Hypothèques* may be created over ships and inland waterway craft (barges), and to be effective against third parties they must be registered at the port registry or the inland waterways registry where the ships or barges are registered. Aircraft may be charged by *hypothèques* which are registered in the national aircraft register. All such *hypothèques* are enforceable by judicial orders for the sale of the ships, barges or aircraft and the appropriate distribution of the proceeds of sale.

Secondly, a wide range of goods and equipment, used or resold in connection with businesses, may be charged with indebtedness for loans or otherwise by using a document representing the goods as though it were the goods themselves and delivering the document to the pledgee. This may be done, as in English law, by pledging bills of lading relating to the goods carried by sea (*connaissements*), and since the extension in 1960 of the rules governing bills of lading to the transportation of goods by inland waterway, it would seem that pledges over goods being transported by canal can be created by delivery of an inland waterway company's bill of lading to the pledgee. Whether consignment notes in respect of goods carried by land (*lettres de voiture*) and air waybills (*lettres de transport áerien*) may similarly be used to create pledges over the goods to which they relate is doubtful.

Thirdly, in addition to pledges of goods by the delivery of a transportation document to the pledgee, French legislation also permits the creation of pledges of certain classes of goods by the issue of two-part documents in respect of them by the person who has physical possession of them or by a public registry. The first part of the document (the *warrant*) represents the right to the delivery of the goods, and the other (the *récépissé*) acknowledges their custody by the issuer of the document or by a specified person or company. The *warrant* is capable of transfer by endorsement and delivery to a third person, thus transferring the right to delivery of the goods, and if the warrant is delivered to a lender or creditor for the purpose of creating a security over the goods, a pledge over them arises on the endorsement and delivery of the warrant to him. A register of such warrants must be kept by the issuer of them, but this plays no part in determining the validity or priority of claims made in respect of the goods. A lender or creditor who is secured by the endorsement and delivery to him of a *warrant* is protected by the fact that the issuer of the document, or the person specified in it as the possessor of the goods, may not lawfully deliver them to anyone other than the holder or endorsee of the document on its surrender to the possessor. In the meantime the possessor holds the goods on behalf of the holder or latest endorsee, who is therefore treated as being in possession of them indirectly and, if he is a lender on the security of the goods, as having a pledge over them.

The earliest legislation enabling goods to be pledged by means of the *warrant-récépissé* related to goods stored in general warehouses which accepted goods or goods of a particular class or classes from anyone on deposit (*magasins généraux*). The availability of the document as a means of enabling a succession of persons to have indirect possession of goods and to pledge them, has by subsequent piecemeal legislation been extended to agricultural produce (including growing crops), equipment used in carrying on a hotel business or any other businesses (in the latter case the equipment must bear a plaque indicating the pledgee's interest), unsold stocks of manufactured products, and stocks of imported petroleum. Where the pledgor is in physical possession of the goods in question (as in the case of agricultural produce, equipment used in a business, and stocks of manufactured products) the document used to effect the pledge is simply a *warrant,* no *récépissé* being necessary, and the pledgee is protected by the issue of the warrant being registered at the local civil or commercial court registry.

Fourthly, under legislation enacted in 1909, it is possible for the owner of a business (*fonds de commerce*) to create a charge (*nantissement*) over it by an agreement which is registered at the local commercial court. By charging the business, the agreement effectively creates a security in favour of the lender or creditor over the goodwill and trade connection of the business, over its business name, and over the owner's right to any lease he holds of the premises where the business is carried on and to its renewal. By express mention the charge may be extended to the plant and equipment of the business, to patents and trade marks held in connection with it, and to exploitation concessions held by it (for example, mining, quarrying and oil exploitation licences). However, the charge may not be extended to raw materials, finished and semi-finished goods, or stock in trade. The distinguishing features of the charge over a business are that it is given over the constituent items of the business mentioned above as they exist from time to time, and not merely over those constituents which are comprised in the business at the time the charge is created. The owner of the business remains in possession of the charged items, and on giving notice of his intention to the secured creditor has full power to dispose of them in carrying on the business until the secured lender or creditor takes enforcement proceedings.

The contractual charge created over a business resembles the floating charge created by an English company over its assets and undertaking, but it differs from such a charge because it extends only to certain classes of assets comprised in the business, and the only way in which the charge may be realised (since it is not a pledge) is by judicial sale. A judicial sale may also be applied for by a judgment creditor of the owner of the business or by an unpaid vendor of the business to the owner, and such a judgment creditor or vendor may register a charge (*privilège*) over the assets of the business at the local commercial court to secure his claim. The order for sale obtained by a creditor who has a charge on a business, or by a judgment creditor or unpaid vendor extends to the whole of the assets of the business, but a creditor who has a charge on the business is entitled to payment of the amount secured only out of the proceeds of those assets of the business which were subject to his charge. Priority for payment out of the proceeds is determined as between such persons according to the order in which their respective charges were registered. The contractual charge (*nantissement*) of a business is widely used to create security over small- and medium-sized businesses, but it is rarely used to secure loans made to large public companies. Its practical significance is therefore much less than that of the English floating charge.

Competing claims for priority over pledges of tangible moveables

One of the disadvantages of the pledge as a security under French law is that the creditor secured by it has to face the competition of competing claims by other creditors on whom the law confers general or special liens or charges (*privilèges*) for what would otherwise be unsecured debts. The general liens or charges rank in the order in which the relevant legislation lists them, and include:

(a) the privilege of the state for unpaid taxes and customs duties accruing during the preceding two years;
(b) the primary or 'superprivilege' of employees and commercial agents in insolvency proceedings for a limited amount of salaries and other remuneration owed to them;
(c) the expenses of judicial proceedings taken by any creditor for the benefit of all the creditors of the debtor; and

(d) the unpaid remuneration of employees which is not covered by the superprivilege.

The special liens or charges created by law extend only to particular assets of the debtor, and include the lien of:

(a) a lessor over goods from time to time brought on to the premises leased by him;
(b) an unpaid seller of goods over those goods;
(c) a person who has preserved goods from loss or destruction for the expenses incurred in doing so; and
(d) carriers of goods for unpaid freight or carriage charges.

The order in which general and special liens or charges over goods arising by law rank in relation to pledges of the goods has never been conclusively determined by the French courts. Nevertheless, general liens or charges are postponed to pledges if the pledgee took delivery of the goods comprised in his pledge without being aware of the existence of the general lien or charge in question. It also seems that in the absence of legislation to the contrary, such general liens or charges are postponed to pledges in other cases (including *gages sans déplacement* and *nantissements de fonds de commerce*) on the wider principle that general liens or charges arising by operation of law cannot displace specific securities over particular assets, although some French courts have rejected such a principle. As regards special liens and charges arising by law, the better view seems to be that a pledge has priority over all such liens or charges, whenever arising, except those of a lessor, or an unpaid seller of the goods to the pledgor of whose claim the pledgee was aware, and of a person who has preserved the goods from loss or destruction after the pledge was created. The weakness of French law in this respect is that, unlike English law, it recognises general and special liens over goods arising by operation of law even though the person claiming the lien does not have possession of the goods, and it does not make good this deficiency by providing for the registration of non-possessory liens.

Pledges and securities over intangible moveables

French law permits pledges to be created over debts and rights against third parties (whether arising from contracts or otherwise) (*créances*) and over industrial property rights and investments (shares and bonds issued by companies). The procedures are the same as for the assignment of such rights, except that pledges over investments in bearer form are created in the same way as pledges over tangible moveables (that is, by delivery of the investment certificate to the pledgee or to a custodian nominated by him). Pledges over all other intangible moveables are created therefore by an agreement between the pledgor and pledgee which is formally notified by a court official (*huissier*) serving a copy of the agreement (*exploit*) on the debtor or other person against whom the pledged rights exist, or by the latter acknowledging by a notarial act that he accepts the existence of the pledge. Alternatively, pledges of industrial property rights may be created by written agreements or notarial acts which are noted on the national register of patents, trade marks or designs (as the case may be). Pledges or charges over shares in registered form issued by public companies may be created by written transfers expressed to be by way of security (*transfert de garantie*) which are entered in the share register kept by the issuing company.

Because the transfer or pledge of debts (particularly trade debts for goods or services supplied) involves considerable formality and expense, the usual practice is for transfers and pledges to be effected by contractual subrogation (*subrogation conventionelle*); that is, by an agreement between the assignor and assignee, or the pledgor and the pledgee, that the assignee or pledgee shall be substituted for the assignor or pledgor in his relation to the debtor. Such an arrangement is possible under French law, though not under English or German law, which recognise subrogation only by operation of law (for example on a guarantor discharging the debt he has guaranteed, or an insurance company making a payment in respect of an insured loss for which the policyholder has a claim against a third person). The effect of a contractual subrogation under French law is that the beneficiary of the subrogation succeeds to the rights of the original creditor as they exist at the time when the subrogation is notified orally or in writing to the debtor liable in respect of the subrogated claim. Priority between successive subrogations of the same debt or claim is governed by the order in which the subrogation agreements are made, whereas successive formal assignments or pledges of debts or other rights rank in the order they are formally notified to, or accepted by, the debtor or other person who is liable to satisfy the claim, because until that is done the assignment or pledge is incomplete.

A more direct alternative method by which commercial companies may assign or pledge trade debts owed to them in order to raise finance for their operations from banks and financial institutions has been provided by legislation enacted in 1981. Instead of a contractual subrogation, the company executes a simplified form of assignment or charge to the financing institution, accompanied by a signed and dated list of the trade debts comprised in the transfer or charge. The assignee or chargee may notify the debtors and require them to pay their debts directly to it (although this is not necessary for the validity of the assignment or charge), or it may permit the company to collect the debts itself and apply them for the benefit of the assignee or chargee. If the debtors are notified of the assignment or charge, and are required to pay their debts to the financing institution, they must do so, but they may rely on any defences which they could have raised at the time of the notification if an action had then been brought by the company against them. Priorities between successive assignees or chargees of the same debts are determined by the order in which their respective assignments or charges were executed.

French law does not provide for the registration of intangible moveables (other than industrial property rights and investments in registered form), or for the registration of assignments of them, or of the creation of pledges or charges over them, unless they relate to intangible moveables which are themselves registered.

Pledges and other securities over intangible moveables are enforceable in the same way as such securities over tangible moveables, namely by judicial sale, or if the transaction effecting the pledge or charge is commercial in character, by sale on the initiative of the pledgee or chargee. The rules governing the application of the proceeds of sale and the priorities between the claims of the pledgee or chargee and the claims of persons entitled to general or special liens or charges over the intangibles by operation of law are the same as in respect of tangible moveables. Alternatively, if the intangibles which are subject to a pledge or charge created contractually are debts, the pledgee or chargee who has notified the debtor (formally by an *exploit* served by a *huissier*, or informally if the charge was effected by contractual subrogation, or by an informal transfer of trade debts under the legislation of 1981), the pledgee or chargee may recover the debts by suing the debtors directly when their debts become due.

German law

The German Civil Code recognises the pledge (*Pfandrecht*) as the standard form of security for debts and money claims which may be created over both tangible and intangible moveables. However, because of developments in the law by judicial decision since the Civil Code came into operation in 1900, the pledge is not now the principal form of security which is used, and has been largely supplanted in practice by the security transfer (*Sicherungsübereignung, Sicherungsabtretung*).

Pledges and securities over tangible moveables

A pledge is created under the terms of the German Civil Code by an agreement to create it as a security for any claim of the pledgee against the pledgor or a third person (not necessarily a money claim) accompanied by the pledgee being put into possession or already having possession of the goods pledged, or by the goods being in joint possession of the pledgor and the pledgee (thus facilitating their continued use by the pledgor). The possession of the pledgee may be direct or indirect; direct possession is physical possession whereas indirect possession is physical possession by a third person who undertakes to hold the goods at the disposal of the pledgee. If possession of the goods, whether direct or indirect, is returned to the pledgor with the consent of the pledgee, the pledge ceases to exist. The remedy of the pledgee, if the claim which the pledge secures is not discharged in accordance with the contract or other transaction creating it, is to sell the pledged goods by public auction and to discharge the claim or its value out of the proceeds of sale. No court order is required for the pledgee to exercise his power of sale, but he must give the pledgor one month's warning of his intention to do so after the power of sale has arisen. Any provision in the contract for the pledge that the pledgee shall become, or may acquire the right to become, the owner of the goods pledged on the pledgor's default is void, but this does not prevent the pledgee from buying the goods from the pledgor by a separate transaction after the pledge has been created.

The form of security over tangible moveables which has practically supplanted the pledge, the security transfer (*Sicherungsübereignung*), has been achieved by the use of a provision in the Civil Code by which (as an exception to the general rule that ownership of goods can only be transferred by an agreement to transfer it, coupled with the delivery of direct or indirect possession of the goods to the transferee) an owner of goods may transfer ownership by agreeing to do so and at the same time declaring that he retains the direct or indirect possession of the goods for and at the disposal of the transferee (*Besitzkonstitut*). This cannot be done under French law, and the nearest equivalent to it under English law is an owner agreeing to transfer ownership (for valuable consideration if the agreement is not by deed) and attorning or declaring that he retains possession as a bailee for the transferee. The German Civil Code provides that this method of transferring ownership may be used to pass absolute, unconditional ownership (for example, on a sale or gift). However, in the early 1900s, the German Supreme Court declared that it could also be used when a condition subsequent is attached to the transfer, namely, in the case of a security transaction, that the transferred ownership shall revest in the transferor if and when the secured debt is paid or the secured obligation is fulfilled. Thus was born the German mortgage of goods (transfer by way of security), and by its use the need for the delivery to, and retention of, possession of the goods by the lender or his custodian, or by the lender and the borrower jointly (which was required for a pledge) was avoided.

The usefulness of the security transfer of goods was increased by subsequent decisions of the German Supreme Court which recognised such a transfer as valid even if the goods to which it related did not exist or were not owned by the transferor when the agreement for the transfer was made. This was so, provided that the goods or the class to which they belonged were adequately specified in the agreement, and the ownership of the goods by way of security then vested in the transferee immediately on the transferor acquiring them. Later court decisions also recognised the security transfer as valid, if it was made to secure loans to or debts of the transferor to be incurred in the future after the agreement for the transfer was made. This is so even if the transferee gives no commitment to make the loans or to give credit to the transferee. Consequently, an agreement by a business customer of a bank to transfer the whole of his present and future stock in trade to the bank as security for the amount for the time being overdrawn on his account, and to hold possession of the stock in trade for the bank as its owner until the account is closed with no debit balance on it, creates a valid security. The bank immediately becomes the owner on security (*sicherungshalber*) of the stock which the customer owns at the time the agreement is made, and it will also become the owner on security of all stock which the customer later acquires on his acquiring it.

If the security were left in the form of a global transfer of present and future current assets of a business, the customer would, of course, not be able to dispose of any of his stock in trade in the course of carrying on his business. The security agreement therefore usually permits him to do this, but provides that the trade debts owed to him by his customers for stock which he sells them shall be automatically vested in the bank (*Vorausabtretung*), and that the customer shall collect those debts as the bank's agent and shall pay the proceeds into his bank account to reduce his indebtedness. By this means a bank can safely finance the current trading of a business customer and have a valid, continuing and automatically effective security over the whole of his current stock in trade and trade debts, or, if the customer is a manufacturer, over his or its raw materials, semi-finished and finished products, and the proceeds of their eventual sale to customers. The Germans know this secured financing arrangement as a *Globalzession*, and its usefulness is undoubted. Its weakness lies in the fact that there is no system of registration for security transfers of goods and the proceeds of selling them. When account is taken of the almost universal practice of sellers of goods in Germany to reserve the ownership of the goods to themselves after delivery to the purchaser until the price or the current indebtedness of the purchaser to the seller is discharged, but to permit resales by the purchaser subject to the resale price belonging to the unpaid seller, it can be seen that the potential for conflicting claims to priority by banks and unpaid sellers is considerable.

The German *Globalzession* fulfils the same function as the English floating charge created over a class of a company's assets, but it differs in law from the floating charge in two respects. In the first place the *Globalzession* is, in English terms, a mortgage (a security transfer) and not a charge in the English equity sense; British borrowers mortgage their land and charge their moveables, whereas German borrowers do the converse. Secondly, of more practical importance, a German bank will lend on the security of a transfer of a company's present and future stock in trade and trade debts, but not on the security of the whole of its present and future assets and undertaking. This is because under the German Civil Code a person who takes a transfer of the whole, or substantially the whole, of the assets of another becomes personally liable to pay all the other person's debts outstanding at the time of the transfer. This provision is designed to protect individuals from their overweening creditors (particularly moneylenders), but it also applies to companies. German banks are therefore careful to confine their security to a part only of their corporate customers' assets so as to avoid changing their status from that of secured creditors to statutory guarantors. Furthermore, the German courts have held that if a creditor of a business undertaking, whether corporate or not, takes an excessive security over its assets, so that it is left with an inadequate residue of assets to offer as security to other lenders and creditors in order to raise the finance which it needs, the excessive security is void because taking it is contrary to good business ethics (*sittenwidrig*), a ground for invalidity under the German Civil Code.

Because of the availability of the security transfer of tangible moveables and its advantages over the pledge, it has become the standard form of security required by lenders, and the pledge has fallen into disuse. Because of this, German law has not needed to evolve the variant kinds of security over tangible moveables which piecemeal legislation has created in France. Nevertheless, there is one variant kind of security in German law which may be used only in respect of certain classes of tangible moveables and which is still used because of the advantages it has over the security transfer. It is the *Hypothek* or security charge which may be created over ships (whether complete or in the course of construction), inland waterway craft and aircraft. The legislation governing *Hypotheken* over such assets applies to the provisions governing security charges over land (with a few exceptions), substituting the national shipping registry at the principal North Sea ports of Germany, the internal waterways registries in the canalised zone of Germany and the national aircraft registry at Frankfurt for the local land registries.

Pledges and securities over intangible moveables

A pledge over rights unconnected with land, that is a pledge of contractual and other obligations and liabilities, or of industrial and property rights or investments, may be created under German law by an agreement between the pledgor and pledgee which in form would be sufficient to effect a transfer of the rights. Since a claim may be transferred by an agreement in any form (even oral), no formalities are required for such a pledge. The pledge is complete on the making of the agreement, and notification of the debtor or any person who is responsible for fulfilment of the pledged obligation, liability or right is not necessary to constitute the pledge or to preserve priority for the pledgee. Notice of a pledge of patent rights must, however, be given to the Patent Office and entered in the register of patents. If no notice of the pledge is given to the person under the obligation or liability or against whom the right may be enforced, and he satisfies the obligation or right by making payment or rendering performance to the pledgor in ignorance of the pledge, the obligation or right is discharged as regards the pledgee as well as the pledgor. Exceptionally, a pledge of a right secured by an instrument which is transferable by endorsement (for example, a bill of exchange or a share certificate in respect of registered shares of a public company) must be completed by delivery of the endorsed instrument to the pledgee. A pledge of an instrument in bearer form (for example, a bearer bond) is effected by the delivery of the instrument to the pledgee as security for an obligation, and the pledge is governed by the rules relating to pledges of tangible moveables as though the instrument embodied the rights it represents.

The obligation comprised in a pledge can be discharged by the debtor or obligee who is subject to it making payment or rendering performance to the pledgor and pledgee jointly. However, if the obligation or liability to secure which the pledge was given has fallen due for performance, the pledgee may enforce the pledged obligation without the concurrence of the pledgor. A pledge becomes enforceable when the obligation or liability which it secures falls due. Enforcement is by judicial proceedings brought by the pledgee against the debtor or obligor whose debt or obligation is comprised in the pledge. If the pledged obligation is a debt, the court orders its payment to the pledgee when it falls due. If it is any other obligation, the court orders that it shall be performed toward the pledgee and not the pledgor. If the rights which are pledged are investments (for example, shares or bonds) or industrial property rights, the court may order their sale and the payment of sufficient of the proceeds to the pledgee to settle the liability for which the pledge was given. As in respect of pledges of tangible moveables, any provision in a pledge agreement which enables the pledgee to acquire the right which has been pledged as his own property on the pledgor's default is void.

The pledge of intangible moveables, like that of tangibles, has been largely replaced by the security transfer (*Sicherungsabtretung*), by which the person entitled to the right given as security, transfers it to the lender or creditor on terms that the right shall revest in him when the debt or other obligation for which the security is given is discharged. The remarks made above in respect of security transfers of tangible moveables apply equally to security transfers of intangibles. The rights transferred as security may comprise rights acquired by the person who gives the security in the future as well as rights he already has, provided the future rights are defined sufficiently clearly for it to be certain whether they are included in the security transfer when they are acquired (for example, the present and future trade debts of a specified business). Moreover, security transfers of intangibles may be given to secure both present and future indebtedness, and may therefore be given to secure the amount from time to time owing to a bank on its customer's current account. In fact, the security transfer of the whole of the present and future trade debts owed to a business (*Globalzession*) is a common form of security for the continued bank financing of a business. This applies whether standing alone or given in conjunction with a security transfer of the stock in trade, or finished or semi-finished products, of a business.

Priorities

The elasticity and wide availability of the security transfer of tangible and intangible moveables has made it unnecessary for German law to elaborate the varying forms of security which have been provided by legislation in France as an alternative to the pledge. The one handicap which German law suffers, however, is that because security transfers are not explicitly recognised by the German Civil Code, there are no enacted rules to govern conflicting claims to priority for different securities over the same tangible or intangible moveables, and no system for registering security transfers so as to determine priorities. Priority rules have therefore been worked out by judicial decisions which have applied the priority rules applicable to pledges by analogy. Basically, security transfers rank for priority in the order in which they are created, and this is so whether the security interests are claimed in respect of moveables owned or vested in the transferor at the dates of the respective security transfers, or in respect of moveables subsequently acquired by him. The basic order of priority may be displaced, however, if it is the usual practice in the trade or business carried on by the transferor for short-term, current indebtedness to be secured by particular forms of security. In this case a security transferee who makes a long-term loan or provides continuing or revolving credit facilities (for example, a bank which finances the transferor's current trading by overdraft facilities), may have his security postponed to such particular securities for short-term indebtedness which the transferor later creates. Consequently, in classes of business where it is customary for sellers to supply goods to trade purchasers on credit and to retain the ownership of the goods supplied until they are paid for, but to permit the purchasers to resell the goods on condition that the resale prices shall belong to the unpaid sellers (extended retention of title or *verlängerter Eigentumsvorbehalt*), a bank which has taken a global security transfer of all the purchaser's trade debts, present and future, before goods are sold to him on those conditions cannot assert priority for its global security over the resale prices of such goods, but must submit to the proceeds of those resales being applied first in paying what is owed to the unpaid sellers. Moreover, the basic order of priority determined by the chronological order in which securities over moveables are created may give way when a creditor whose security was created first has taken an excessive security for the amounts which are in the event owed to him. This results in the owner of the assets comprised in the security having insufficient other assets left to use as security for other debts he incurs or is likely to incur in carrying on his business. The excessive security is then void because it is contrary to good business ethics (*sittenwidrig*), and the later security consequently gains priority. Because of this, prior securities for amounts which vary over time (for example, the amount owing to a bank on an overdrawn account) are usually limited by the agreement to comprise only assets whose value at the time they are acquired will not make the value of all the assets then subject to the security exceed 120 or 140 % of the total indebtedness which is then secured, or some other appropriate percentage of that amount (the *Freigabeklausel*). If the agreed percentage provides only a reasonable margin for credit risks and contingencies (for example, a falling market), the security will not be excessive, and the German courts have held that it will be valid despite the complexity of the necessary calculations.

CONCLUSION

The foregoing survey will have shown that there are major differences between the different legal systems of Member States of the European Communities governing the kinds of securities over land and moveables which they respectively recognise and between the legal rules which apply to such securities. In view of these differences, any attempt to harmonise or approximate the laws of the different countries will be beset with almost insurmountable difficulties. Even the introduction of a standard registration system so as to provide publicity for securities and to determine priorities between them would probably founder because the underlying property law systems of the Member States are so divergent. The only attempt which has so far been made toward harmonisation of national laws in this area is in respect of retention of title clauses in agreements for the sale of goods, and that was confined to simple retention of title provisions which do not extend to the proceeds of resale.

The prognosis for harmonisation is poor, but before attempting it, it is worthwhile asking whether it is necessary or even desirable. With regard to securities over land, the attempt would not seem likely to result in any material advantages, particularly in view of the fact that only one system of law can apply to a mortgage or charge over land during the whole time it exists. Again, the law governing securities over intangibles could be simplified or made clearer in many Member States. However, such securities are at least subject to only one system of law during the whole of the time they exist, namely, the law of the country in which the intangible is treated as situate, and the laws of the Member States are fairly uniform on the proper location of intangibles.

Securities over tangible moveables present serious practical problems because of the inter-state mobility of goods, however, and the approximation of the laws of Member States in respect of securities over goods which are traded internationally would provide considerable advantages. Nevertheless, there must be major doubts as to the practicability of such an approximation in view of the present extreme diversity of national laws.

7—PAYMENT AND CLEARING SYSTEMS IN THE EUROPEAN COMMUNITY

Ross Cranston

Payment systems are the instruments, rules and procedures that enable users to meet payment obligations. Even if a payment obligation must ultimately be met in legal tender, parties can forgo this right and agree to other ways of meeting the obligation.[1] Claims on banks are commonly used to meet payment obligations. Traditionally, payment systems are classified as credit or debit transfers, depending on whether the payor's payment instructions are given direct to its bank (credit transfer) or pass via the payee (a debit transfer). Payment systems are either paper based, electronic, or a combination of both. An additional classification used below divides payment systems into consumer and commercial systems; to some extent this mirrors the accepted division between retail and commercial banking.

Payment systems operate by the payor instructing its bank to pay the payee. If both parties have their accounts with the same bank, payment can be made by an adjustment of the accounts. The payment either creates a new debt owed by the payor to the bank, or discharges or reduces an existing debt the bank owes to the payor. At the same time payment discharges the payor's obligation to the payee. The bank is now obliged to the payee, or the payee's debt to the bank is reduced. Additional parties do not affect this basic method of how payment is effected. Where payor and payee have different banks, say in different countries, the payor's bank instructs the payee's bank to pay the payee, and in the process becomes indebted to that other bank.[2]

Settlement between the payor and the payee's bank could be through a settlement account maintained for that purpose, or across the books of the central bank. With international payments, each

1. *Libyan Arab Foreign Bank* v *Bankers Trust Co.* [1988] 1 Lloyd's Rep 259; [1987] 2 FTLR 509.
2. See B. Geva, 'The Concept of Payment Mechanisms' (1986) 24 *Osgoode H.L.J.* 1.

bank may maintain a correspondent account for the other. Where the banks are not linked in this way, they may well use a third, a correspondent bank to this end. Alternatively, they may be linked to a network providing settlement facilities. The number of banks involved in any payment depends on whether and how the banks are linked through such settlement systems.

Because there is likely to be a string of payments between particular banks, it is sensible to net or clear payments on a regular basis. Clearing systems operate to net the credit and debit transactions, or to settle the final balances of any intermediate clearing. As the Bank for International Settlements puts it:

> 'This need calls for a system with highly specialised instruments and procedures, and one to which only a restricted circle of users has access. It is worth mentioning that at this level the means of settlement must be acceptable to all participants and must also be freely and readily acceptable to the central banks.[3]

Finally, mention should be made of message systems which are analytically distinct from payment and clearing systems. These are designed to provide a secure method for transferring payment instructions. SWIFT, based in Brussels, is the best known of the international message systems.[4]

EUROPEAN PAYMENT AND CLEARING SYSTEMS

Each European country has its domestic payment and clearing systems. For example, each has a system for clearing cheques and debit and credit transfers, although the extent and operation of these varies considerably. However, there are also payment and clearing systems which have a cross-border character. At the retail level, the best known is the Eurocheque system, although as important are the global card systems—for example, Visa and Mastercard/Access/Eurocard—which obviously have a European dimension. Postal Giro systems are also used, although to a more limited extent.

At the commercial level, the domestic systems have international, and hence European, implications. If, say, a German bank wants

3. *Systeme des Zahlungsverkehrs in elf Industrieländern*, Frankfurt, Fritz Knapp Verlag, 1980, p.5.
4. For example, P. Frazer, *Plastic and Electronic Money*, Cambridge, Woodhouse-Faulkner, 1985, Appendix A4; A. Lipis, *et al*, *Electronic Banking*, New York, John Wiley, 1985, pp.182–7.

to pay sterling to an Italian company it will probably instruct its London correspondent to pay the Italian company's bank through the latter's London correspondent. The transfer between the London correspondents will be effected through one of the London payment and clearing systems, such as CHAPS.[5] Similarly, if the German bank had wanted to pay French francs, a French payment and clearing system such as SAGITTAIRE may have been used. While domestic systems may have European implications, there are commercial payment and clearing systems which are European in character. First, there is the Currency Clearing scheme in London, through which certain cheques and banker's drafts in European currencies can be cleared. Secondly, there is the ECU clearing and settlement system set up by the ECU Banking Association. Thirdly, there are the clearing systems for the international trade in securities, which can also be used, directly and indirectly, to effect payment.

Eurocheque

Eurocheque is an international payment system established in 1968 at the initiative of European banks. There are some 40 European and Mediterranean countries with participants, including the Community countries. Active participants issue cheques and cheque guarantee cards to their customers; passive participants do not themselves issue cheques and cards but cash guaranteed cheques at their counters. There is an identical format for the guaranteed Eurocheque and for the guarantee card. The administration of the Eurocheque scheme throughout Europe is the responsibility of the Eurocheque Assembly (members are national organisations representing their member banks) and Eurocheque International (the secretariat).[6]

Eurocheques may be made out in the currency of any of the member countries, and may be used not merely to obtain currency from banks, to make payments abroad, or to make payments to third parties abroad, but also to make payments in the home country. Eurocheques written abroad go to a Eurocheque centre in that country, which sends them, or information about them, to the centre in the country of the drawee bank. The clearing centre of the payee bank debits the account which the clearing centre

5. In the event that both the German and Italian banks have the same London correspondent, there will be no need, of course, to use a payment and clearing system.
6. 'Statutes of the Eurocheque Community' in *Eurocheque Handbook*, Brussels, Eurocheque, looseleaf.

of the drawee bank has with it. A value of two working days after the date of dispatch is applied to the debits (two working days after receipt of a telex advice for a large remittance).[7] The customer's account is debited in the ordinary way within the drawee country. Unpaid cheques are returned to the collecting bank by the same route as they followed for presentation. The collecting bank then deals with the drawee bank directly. The latter must provide evidence that the cheque has not been accepted in accordance with the Eurocheque Encashment Regulations for banks or the acceptance instructions for retailers.

A form of cheque truncation is common throughout participating countries, in that the cheques themselves are retained at the clearing centres and the information about them sent to each paying bank. Because the cheques themselves are not returned to the paying bank, they could be returned unpaid long after the time normally applicable under domestic cheque clearing rules. As long as the conditions of the Eurocheque card are complied with, however, the drawee bank must pay a Eurocheque because it has guaranteed payment. More importantly, truncation means that there may not be compliance with s. 45 of the United Kingdom Bills of Exchange Act 1882, which requires presentment of a bill (including a cheque) for payment, unless there is waiver of presentment, express or implied. In an arbitration between the Bank of England and members of the committee of London clearing banks, Bingham J. said that presentment for payment required physical delivery of a cheque to the branch of the bank on which it is drawn.[8] To overcome this, conditions of use for Eurocheques issued by some, but not all, UK banks contain a waiver of presentment; the customer agrees to its bank paying the cheque, although it is not presented to the branch on which it is drawn. Any problems posed by the Bills of Exchange Act are thereby avoided. Contrast the Geneva Uniform Law on Cheques: presentment of a bill at a clearing house is equivalent to a presentment for payment.[9]

Payment cards

There is no European payment card as such. However, a number of developments mean that certain payment cards can be used, in effect, throughout the Community. Of course, for some time,

7. *Eurocheque Clearing Handbook*, Brussels, Eurocheque, looseleaf, Section A.
8. *Barclays Bank plc* v *Bank of England* [1985] 1 All ER 385.
9. Art. 31. The Uniform Law requires presentment within 21 days (art. 29), but in practice this is met.

certain credit cards have been usable in this way. More recently, agreements between banks enable customers to use their existing ATM cards at banks in European countries other than their own. One such agreement is associated with Eurocheque cards; the cards are valid for international use throughout the Eurocheque ATM network. Another operates under the Visa logo, being between the Visa card issuing banks. Yet another is operated by Access/Eurocard/Mastercard; Access cardholders, for example, can use their cards in a large number of ATMs located in Spain.

The Visa system is illustrative for present purposes. Visa is an international payment system owned by over 2500 banks in the European, Middle East and African region (20000 worldwide).[10] Member banks enter into direct relationships with customers and merchants. They also contract with Visa itself. Within the system, an issuing bank can offer a range of services – charge cards, credit cards, direct debit cards, or cash dispenser and now EFTPOS cards. The Visa infrastructure gives wide acceptance to a card and customer access to a European payment system. One of Visa's computer systems enables each bank member to seek authorisation on a card issued by any other member. The system either routes the request for authorisation to the card issuer or responds on the card issuer's behalf using predetermined limits. Another computer system is for clearing and settlement: each member can clear and settle financial data with other members six days a week. Clearing and settlement is on a multi-currency basis, allowing transactions to be converted from the currency of purchase into the cardholder's billing currency. Both authorisations and settlements are processed via London.

Currency clearing in London

The London currency settlement scheme originated as the London US dollar clearing in 1975, to enable dollar cheques and drafts in London to be cleared on a same date basis. Clearing now extends to European currencies – the Deutschmark, the French franc, the Italian lira, and the Dutch guilder. The system was conceived as applying to retail payments, that is excluding large interbank and Eurodollar payments. Indeed in June 1981 a 'Working Party on Wholesale Dollar Clearing', set up with the Bank of England and representatives from the banking associations, concluded that there should not be a wholesale dollar clearing in London. The credit risk of a wholesale clearing was one consideration in this conclusion. Now the rules of the London Currency Clearing specifically exclude

10. Visa is worldwide; what follows, concentrates on the European dimension.

cheques drawn in settlement of interbank foreign exchange deals and for principal amounts of interbank Eurocurrency transactions.[11]

The system provides for a clearing of cheques and bankers' payments and drafts in the various currencies paid into and drawn on participating banks throughout the UK. Direct access to the system is limited to seven settlement banks, but there are some 20 other participating banks which have agency arrangements with a settlement bank. Not all participating banks participate in all currencies. Each settlement bank nominates a branch to act as its co-ordinating branch and as agent for the participating banks. The settlement banks each act by rotation as settlement agent for the other settlement banks. Settlement between the settlement agent and the others is effected through specified correspondent banks in the country of the currency: settlement members having to pay the settlement agent instruct their correspondent in sufficient time for value to be obtained in cleared funds according to the timetable. Similarly, the settlement agent instructs its foreign correspondent to pay the receiving settlement members in sufficient time for value to be obtained in cleared funds according to the timetable.[12] Net settlement between the clearing banks and their participant banks is a matter of individual negotiation.

The timetable for the clearing of the European currencies under the rules is that participating banks and branches of the settlement banks cannot accept items from customers, and banker's payments from other banks, after 10 a.m. and must lodge them with the co-ordinating branches by 10.30 a.m. for physical exchange at the Bankers' Clearing House at 11 a.m. Settlement transfers must be dispatched to the correspondent banks in the currency of origin to obtain value in cleared funds two days after the date of exchange. Unpaid and wrongly delivered items must be notified or returned in the time specified by the rules, and are adjusted in later clearings by use of claim vouchers.[13]

ECU clearing

Originally, settlement of ECU payments was through banks opening mutual ECU accounts with each other. The final settlement of the balances was made in the component currencies through the bank

11. Clearing House Rules for the Currency Clearing, rule 4. See also *Libyan Arab Foreign Bank* v *Bankers Trust Co.* [1988] 1 Lloyd's Rep 259, at p. 275; [1987] 2 FTLR 509, at p. 525.
12. Rule 7(e)(f).
13. Rule 2(b).

which centralised the settlements for the particular month, each of the participating banks assuming this role of settlement bank. In fact, it was not necessary to have recourse to the component currencies in most cases since the participating banks agreed not to demand coverage automatically below a ceiling of 20 000 000 ECU and by mutual agreement beyond that amount. This system of clearing ECUs was known as the Mutual ECU Settlement Account (MESA).[14]

The clearing of ECUs has now been centralised. The key role has been performed by the ECU Banking Association (EBA), which was formed in September 1985 and comprises commercial banks from Europe as well as the United States and Japan. The European Investment Bank – an institution of the European Community – is also a member. As well as the agreement between members of EBA, the clearing system for ECUs is based on two other contracts: first, between EBA and the Bank for International Settlements, which acts as agent on behalf of EBA; and secondly, a contract between EBA and SWIFT, which undertakes the netting of ECUs and passes the result to each clearing bank in the system and the Bank for International Settlements. There are other relevant contracts; for example, each clearing bank has an ECU account with the Bank for International Settlements and thus a contract with it.

Interbank payments in ECUs routed through SWIFT are identified and the amounts paid to or paid away from each clearing bank total led and netted. Initially, netting is done each day on a preliminary basis. A bank in debit will attempt to cover the debit through market operations; importantly, it is encouraged to obtain ECUs from the clearing banks which are in credit. (The ECU accounts which clearing banks have with the Bank do not earn interest; therefore the banks in credit have an incentive to lend to the banks in debit.) Consequently, ECU balances should be brought down to near equilibrium, subject to remaining technical balances, by the time of final settlement and the Bank for International Settlements completing its movement on each bank's account.[15] Payment to the Bank in the component currencies to cover positions is unnecessary (and impractical). Although a clearing bank cannot overdraw its account with the Bank, if the market is not in a position to provide funds, a clearing bank may use

14. D. Rambure, 'The ECU Clearing and Payment Systems', in R. M. Levich, *ECU European Currency Unit*, London, Euromoney, 1987, p. 35.
15. Ibid, p. 36; G. Dahin, 'ECU Clearing: The State of the Art', *EBA News Letter*, No. 1, June 1987, p. 5.

ECU credit facilities extended by the Bank. Where banks have not confirmed their final balances produced by SWIFT, or where their bank account with the Bank does not have the necessary balance, the Bank can cancel the day's clearing and postpone it to the next day, after withdrawal of the defaulting bank.

Under the agreement with EBA, the Bank for International Settlements is not a lender of last resort, but is simply EBA's agent. This contrasts with the position of central banks in a domestic clearing. Under the agreement, the Bank for International Settlements is not exposed to any kind of risk. If a clearing bank defaults, it is withdrawn from the clearing before its final completion. SWIFT also is not exposed to great liability; under its agreement with the Association, SWIFT is excluded from responsibility for any loss or damage occurring or arising out of the operation of ECU netting.[16]

Euro-clear

Euro-clear is a settlement system for internationally traded securities. While it is owned by a public limited company registered in the UK, the shares of which are held by over a hundred banks, it is operated in Belgium under contract by Morgan Guaranty Trust Company of New York. Each participant agrees to be bound by the Terms and Conditions Governing Use of Euro-clear and by the Operating Procedures of the Euro-clear System. In the event of a conflict between the Terms and Conditions and Operating Procedures, the former prevail.[17] Both are governed by Belgian law.

In outline, the scheme involves Morgan Guaranty Brussels opening one or more securities clearance accounts, and one or more cash accounts for each participant. A cash account is divided into sub-accounts in each of the 23 currencies and composite currency units available for settlement under the scheme. The securities clearance service is a book entry system, which provides simultaneous exchange of cash and securities on an agreed settlement date. On that date, the securities are transferred by book entry from the securities clearance account of the seller to that of the buyer. Simultaneously, cash is transferred in the agreed currency by book entry from the cash account of the buyer to that of the seller. Obviously the securities settlement service involves

16. Clause 6.2. This agreement is governed by Belgian law. At the time of writing, a new agreement is under negotiation.
17. Operating Procedures, Preface.

payment from one participant to another. However, the cash accounts of participants can also be used for money transfers and banking, although they are primarily designed for the settlement of securities transactions. Payment can be made between participants by book entry; payment can be made from a cash account by transfer to any bank for the account of a named beneficiary; and funds may be deposited for credit to a cash account at correspondents identified for each currency.[18]

THE LAW OF EUROPEAN PAYMENT AND CLEARING SYSTEMS

The various payment and clearing systems outlined are established by one or a number of contracts between customers and banks, between the banks themselves, or between banks and third parties such as retailers. Some of these are formal contracts and provide expressly for a governing law. If not, the governing law must be determined under the rules of private international law obtaining. The governing law determines, of course, the meaning and effect to be given to particular contractual provisions.

Even if there is a governing law for a particular contract, use of a payment or clearing system can involve another system of law. For example, the local law could oblige that customers be provided with certain information whenever they use their Eurocheque or payment card abroad. This would not be inconsistent with Community law; as will be seen, the draft Second Banking Directive permits most Member States to impose conduct of business rules in relation to such matters.

Persons using payment and clearing systems could also commit criminal offences in a Member State other than that of the governing law. For example, an English customer of an English bank who obtains foreign currency at a German bank through use of a Eurocheque or a payment card, when their account is overdrawn and they have no overdraft arrangement, is guilty of obtaining money by deception from the German bank (to use the English terminology for such behaviour). Because that offence is committed abroad, an English court would not have jurisdiction. However, the English Court of Appeal has held that a customer in such circumstances can also be guilty of another offence, obtaining in England a pecuniary advantage by deception in the form of a borrowing by way of overdraft from the bank. The policy behind

18. *Euro-clear*, brochure, Morgan Guaranty Trust Company of New York, 1986, p. 11.

their decision is explicit in the judgment: 'If an English court had no jurisdiction when a person resident here and with a bank account here uses his cheque card abroad dishonestly, a great deal of dishonesty may go unpunished and it may be necessary for Parliament to consider legislation.'[19] This example also illustrates that although the relevant contract might give the answer to many of the problems thrown up by payment and clearing systems, reference must also be made to other areas of law.

Contractual provisions

Any particular payment and clearing system will give rise to a range of contractual relationships. What follows concentrates on a few of the contracts in European payment and clearing systems. It should not be thought that in particular circumstances these will be the only or main contractual provisions. For example, while mention is made of the payor-payor bank relationship, the payor-payee bank relationship may be crucial for a payor seeking compensation for an incorrect payment. The common law does not give a uniform answer to the nature of that relationship.[20]

Payor–payor bank

An example at the retail level is that customers in the UK agree to conditions of use if they apply for and are granted a uniform Eurocheque facility and Eurocheque card. (This contrasts with the situation with ordinary cheque accounts in the UK, where most banks do not seek to impose express conditions of use.) The conditions of use are governed by English law. Typically, they cover many of the problems which could be anticipated by this method of payment. For example, the conditions permit the bank to debit the customer's account for cheques it has paid, and for commission and charges, even if the customer has completed the cheques incorrectly. The way that amounts drawn in another currency are converted into sterling is specified. The customer undertakes not to issue a cheque in excess of the credit balance, unless there is an overdraft, nor to countermand payment.

An example of a contract at the commercial level is that governing the use of the Euro-clear system. As mentioned previously, this

19. *R* v *Bevan* (1987) 84 CAR 143, 148.

20. In English law, there is no privity of contract: *Royal Products Ltd* v *Midland Bank Ltd* [1981] 2 Lloyd's Rep 194, 198. In United States law, a different view might be taken: *Evra Corporation* v *Swiss Bank Corporation* (1982) 673 F2d 951.

is mainly for the clearance of internationally traded securities, but in relation to that payment has to be made through the cash accounts opened for participants, and quite independently these accounts can be used for payments. In relation to movements on the cash accounts, the Terms and Conditions governing use of Euro-clear provide that these are subject to sufficient funds or the provision of such funds being available for any debit to be made. If funds are available to carry out some but not all debits, Morgan Guaranty may determine in its sole discretion which are to be made.[21] In addition, the Terms and Conditions provide that Morgan Guaranty is not required to effect any transaction, or to take any other action, at the demand or upon the instructions of any participant to any extent that this would violate any law of any government, be contrary to any agreement made with Morgan Guaranty, or in other circumstances specified in the Operating Procedures. Morgan Guaranty is exempted from any liability or damage suffered by a participant as a result of this.[22] There is a wide exemption clause.

> In the absence of negligence or wilful misconduct on its part, Morgan Guaranty shall not be liable to any participant or any other person with respect to any action taken or omitted to be taken by it in connection with furnishing the services contemplated hereby and by the Operating Procedures. However, Morgan Guaranty will have no liability to any participant or any other person for indirect or unforeseeable losses, except where such liability is established in the case of gross negligence or wilful misconduct of Morgan Guaranty.[23]

Moreover, a special rule relating to cash accounts provides that except in the case of negligence or wilful misconduct, Morgan Guaranty shall not be liable for delays in carrying out payment instructions given by any participant. The loss which can be claimed in the case of negligence is then specified.[24] In addition, the exemption clause covers verification of the authenticity of instructions, *force majeure* and related events, and loss resulting from a failure by a participant or other person to comply with the procedures or requirements set out in the Operating Procedures. There is also an indemnity clause protecting Morgan Guaranty in the case of a participant failing to comply with any law, contract

21. Clause 6.
22. Clause 7.
23. Clause 12(a).
24. Clause 16(g).

or other instrument binding upon it. Under the Terms and Conditions, Morgan Guaranty can transfer credits between the different currency sub-divisions of an account, and can set-off any credit balance of an account against debts of a participant to other offices of the bank.

Payor bank–payee

Other than for inter-bank payments there will generally be no contract governing payment between the payor's bank and the payee. Despite some ill-considered United States dicta to the contrary,[25] payment is not effected by the assignment of any debt the payor's bank owes the payor.[26] Consequently, payees have no contractual claim on this basis against a payor's bank, but only against their own bank.

Exceptionally, however, there may be special arrangements giving rise to a contract between the payor's bank and the payee. The contract of guarantee which banks enter into with payees of Eurocheques is an example. In English law, the conditions on the Eurocheque card are an offer to the world, which particular payees accept when they take a Eurocheque in accordance with them.[27] (Alternatively, the customer could be regarded as conveying the bank's offer as agent.) One example of the conditions is that the Eurocheque must be signed in the presence of the payee; that the signature must agree with that on the card; that the name of the bank and account on the Eurocheque and on the card must agree; that the number of the card is written on the bank of theEurocheque; and that the Eurocard is issued and dated before the expiry date on the card. Non-compliance with the conditions means that the bank cannot be sued on the guarantee. Under these conditions, if the Eurocheque is used by an imposter, who forges the signature, the signature does not coincide with that on the card, and the payee cannot invoke the guarantee. Typically, the cards themselves do not contain a clause that the guarantee is governed by, for example, English law. Since in the example posited the guarantor is an English bank, and the drawer a customer of an English bank, it is likely that on ordinary principles the proper law of the contract is English law.

25. *Delbrueck & Co.* v *Manufacturers Hanover Trust Company* (1979) 609 F 2d 1047, 1051.

26. *Royal Products Ltd* v *Midland Bank Ltd* [1981] 2 Lloyd's Rep 194, 198. See Dr Mann's discussion in R. Pennington, A. Hudson & E. Mann, *Commercial Banking Law*, Plymouth, Macdonald & Evans, 1978, pp. 285–9.

27. The classic authority is *Carlill* v *Carbolic Smoke Ball Co.* [1893] 1 QB 256. See also *Metropolitan Police Commissioner* v *Charles* [1977] AC 177, 182.

Bank–bank

The third possible contract is between the banks themselves. That contract may be bilateral or multilateral. Correspondent banks clearly enter a bilateral contract with each other. When a payor's bank transfers a payment message to the payee's bank, the latter is bound to effect that message in favour of its customer with due care and skill (which will probably be determined by the ordinary practices of bankers). The payor's bank could claim compensation from the payee's bank were the latter not to meet the requisite standard.

Payment and clearing systems are typically governed by multilateral contracts. The multilateral contract may arise indirectly, in the sense that a contract between a member and a payment and clearing organisation results in a contract among the members as a whole. Alternatively, members of a system may agree together to comply with the rules regarding clearing and settlement. In either event, new members of an existing payment and clearing system will be admitted on the basis of adherence to the existing provisions of the contract.

Traditionally, English law regarded the rules of associations as not being justiciable. The view was that associations were established on a consensual basis, and in the absence of a clear indication that members contemplated the creation of legal relations, their governance was not to be treated as amounting to an enforceable contract.[28] It seems clear, however, that the rules of payment and clearing systems are legally binding – in English law either because in accordance with traditional theory, property rights or the right to trade is involved, or because in terms of basic theory there is an intention to create legal relations. In the case of some payment and clearing systems, it is clear that legal relations are intended, especially if there is an explicit provision for a governing law. Not inconsistently, however, the rules of payment and clearing systems often provide a dispute resolution procedure to avoid resort to the courts. There may be an internal conciliation, and even arbitration procedure, before resort to formal mechanisms is permitted.[29]

Typically, there will be a provision in the payment and clearing

28. For example, see the argument in *Pharmaceutical Society of Great Britain* v *Dickson* [1970] AC 403, 426.

29. For example, the Eurocheque system has a Conciliation Board; its recommendations are published in the *Eurocheque Handbook*. If the parties concerned reject the Conciliation Board's proposal, the Board submits the dispute to the Eurocheque Working Group, which acts as final arbitrator.

rules allowing for their variation from time to time. (In English law, a contract cannot be varied without mutual agreement, but parties can bind themselves to accept variation without such agreement.)[30] At one end of the spectrum, members must accept the variations made by the operator of the system. For example, participants in the Euro-clear system are bound by the Terms and Conditions and Operating Procedures. These may be amended and supplemented at any time upon notice to the participants, and each participant is deemed to have accepted them, effective immediately in the case of any amendment or supplement not adversely affecting participants, or in other cases effective ten business days after notice has been sent.[31] Near the other end of the spectrum, the substance of the rules is democratically decided. For example, the Eurocheque agreement constitutes a Eurocheque assembly, consisting of representatives of participants, which has power to issue and amend rules, but by unanimous vote.[32]

An important question is the extent to which parties which are not members of a payment and clearing system are bound by its rules. The simplest example is where a payor requests its bank to transfer money to a third party – is it bound by the contract between the payor bank and payee bank? Again, will a payee seeking payment on a debit instrument be bound by the contract between payor bank and payee bank in obtaining payment? The answer depends on the circumstances. Certainly it cannot be said that just because the payor and payee are not direct parties to a contract, they are not bound by it because of notions of privity. In English law there is clear authority that one can be bound by the custom and usage of the market, irrespective of one's knowledge of them. Indeed a 'man who employs a banker is bound by the usage of bankers'.[33] The custom or usage becomes binding as an implied term of the payor-bank or payee-bank contract, although where a party is unaware of it the custom or usage can only be implied if it is reasonable.[34] There is some authority treating a rule comparable to a payment and clearing rule as a custom or usage for the purposes of this principle.[35]

30. For example, *Burnett* v *Westminster Bank Ltd* [1966] 1 QB 742.
31. Terms and Conditions, Clauses 3, 19; Operating Procedures, Preface.
32. See footnote 6; arts 10, 15.
33. *Hare* v *Henty* (1861) 142 ER 374, 379.
34. *Sweeting* v *Pearce* (1861) 142 ER 210.
35. *Bell Group Ltd* v *Herald and Weekly Times Ltd* (1985) 9 ACLR 697.

Other areas of law

Contract is at the base of payment and clearing systems. Other areas of law are relevant, however. The law of civil wrongs is one. In England, for largely historical reasons, banks can be strictly liable for the tort of conversion if they collect a cheque, such as a Eurocheque, for other than the true owner. Statute provides some defence.[36] By contrast, in the case of a credit transfer, a payee bank is unlikely to be liable in similar circumstances, unless it has the very high degree of knowledge required in English law of a constructive trustee.[37]

Regulatory law has some bearing on payment and clearing systems. There has been considerable discussion about regulation of the position of consumers in electronic payment systems, although outside the consumer credit area only Denmark has introduced general legislation for payment cards.[38] Less public is the regulatory position regarding payment and clearing systems. There is a potential infringement of national competition law, in so far as the rules of the system are restrictive in their membership and discriminatory in their practices. Because the integrity of payment and clearing systems is crucial to national economic policy, the central bank or another regulatory institution will have at least an informal interest in their operation.

THE ROLE OF COMMUNITY LAW

Certain aspects of Community law bear directly and indirectly on payment and clearing systems. Article 106 of the Treaty provides for the freedom of payments for all transactions that have been liberalised under Community law, thus covering payments for goods and services imported from other Member States. Community law provides for a substantial freedom of movement of capital, although Member States are still able to invoke the protective clauses in the Treaty to maintain restrictions such as exchange control (arts. 73, 108(3)). Where such restrictions do not obtain, individuals and undertakings are able to open bank accounts in other Member States, which they may wish to do for convenience or possibly

36. Cheques Act 1957, s. 4.
37. Constructive knowledge is not enough: *Lipkin Gorman* v *Karpnale Ltd* [1989] FLR 137.
38. See S. Mulvad, 'The Danish Payment Cards Act of 1984', unpublished paper, 1987. There are, of course, specific provisions elsewhere: for example, Banking Act 1987 (UK), s. 88.

to obtain higher returns. Payments of non-residents are thus effected by banks in Member States and processed by their clearing systems.

Three areas of Community law which bear directly on payment and clearing systems are competition law, the draft Second Banking Directive, and the measures taken in relation to payment cards.

Competition law

An aspect of Community law directly relevant to payment and clearing systems is the competition policy embodied in the Treaty. Article 85(1) of the Treaty prohibits agreements between undertakings, decisions by associations of undertakings and concerted practices which may affect trade between Member States which have an anti-competitive effect. Article 85(3) provides, however, that the provisions of para. 1 may be declared inapplicable in the case of:

> — any agreement or category of agreements between undertakings:
> — any decision or category of decisions by associations of undertakings:
> — any concerted practice or category of concerted practices:
> which contributes to improving the production or distribution of goods or to promoting technical or economic progress, while allowing consumers a fair share of the resulting benefit, and which does not:
>
> (a) impose on the undertakings concerned, restrictions which are not indispensable to the attainment of these objectives:
> (b) afford such undertakings the possibility of eliminating competition in respect of a substantial part of the products in question.

Thus, the uniform Eurocheque agreement had to be granted exemption under art. 85(3) by the Commission in relation to the provisions between payee banks and the national clearing banks and between the clearing centres of the various countries.[39] A particular provision approved was that a commission of 1.25% of the amount of the cheque applied to all uniform Eurocheques made out abroad in the local currency, which was to be debited when the cheque was refunded at the clearing centres (rather than at the time of encashment by the cashier or by the retailer when

39. *Re Eurocheques* [1984] 1 CMLR 129.

accepting the cheque). The clearing centre of the payee bank was then to debit the accounts which the clearing centres of other countries had with it with the total amount of the corresponding Eurocheque consignment plus the 1.25%.

The Commission granted the exemption because in its view it was indispensable for the operation of the scheme that there be common terms and conditions for accepting and clearing Eurocheques between issuing and accepting institutions.

> Variations in commissions from one bank to another would imply bilateral negotiations between the 15 000 banks which are parties to the scheme so that each accepting bank (payee bank) may agree with each issuing bank (drawee bank) the remuneration it wishes to receive. Any centralised clearing would thus be made impossible and the cost of processing Eurocheques would substantially increase.[40]

The Commission emphasised that the agreement did not cover the relations between customers and issuing banks and thus the charges which the latter could impose. Consequently, English banks, for example, could charge different amounts for the use of Eurocheques, and competition between them would not be impaired. The Commission imposed as a condition of acceptance that the banks inform their customers in exact detail of any costs which could arise as a result of their use of Eurocheques abroad.

Agreements for the inter-operability of payment card systems will also have to be vetted by the Commission. To satisfy the cumulative requirements of art. 85, it will have to be shown that agreements about inter-operability contribute to promoting technical or economic progress by strengthening the internal market of a people's Europe and implementing industrial policy; allow consumers and traders a fair share of the resulting benefits; impose only indispensable restrictions; and because the possibility remains of users paying by cash or cheque, permit sufficient competition.[41] Inter-operability agreements would seem to have to leave to each card issuer the right to decide on the commission and charges for the service providers and users. Moreover, the insertion of exclusive operation clauses in agreements between card issuers and service

40. *Re Eurocheques* [1985] 3 CMLR 434, 446. See M. Dassesse, 'EEC Competition Law Affecting Banking' [1988] 3 JIBL 105, 108–9. The Eurocheque agreement is again before the Commission for approval.

41. Commission of the European Communities, *Europe Could Play an Ace: The New Payment Cards*, Com (86) 754, 1987, p. 15.

providers would seem to render an agreement incompatible with Treaty rules.

Draft Second Banking Directive[42]

The draft Second Banking Directive also has implications for payment and clearing systems. Among the activities in the annexed list, which credit institutions can freely undertake in other Member States as well as their own, by the establishment of branches or the supply of services, are 'money transmission services' and the 'issuing and administering [of] means of payment (credit cards, traveller's cheques and banker's drafts)'. One difficulty is that the specific mention of 'credit cards, traveller's cheques and banker's drafts' might be taken to exclude other means of payment, but a broader interpretation would regard these as illustrative only.

Under the draft Second Directive, then, it would seem that a payment and clearing system can be made freely available to anyone in the Community. For example, a bank established in one Member State can open an account and issue a cheque book to someone in another Member State, and a bank established in one Member State can open an ATM terminal in another state for use of its customers or others when in that state. But can a bank established in one Member State demand membership of a payment and clearing system in another Member State? It would seem not, unless the payment and clearing system operated a discriminatory policy against banks of another Member State, or unless the restrictions on access fell within the anti-competitive provisions of art. 85. This seems to follow because, although the draft Second Directive ensures that a bank does not need authorisation apart from its home country authorisation to engage in money transmission services and the means of payment, it does not overcome access barriers unless these are in breach of the general principles of Community law.

Article 19 para. 3 of the draft Second Directive allows restrictions by a host state 'justified on the grounds of the public good'. The fourteenth recital in the Preamble is wider in the sense that it speaks of Member States ensuring that there are no obstacles 'to the activities benefitting from mutual recognition being undertaken using the financial techniques of the home Member State, as long as the latter are not in violation of the legal provisions governing the public good in the host Member State'. Since the fourteenth recital is not given force in the text of the Treaty itself, however, regard must be had only to art. 19. The effects of the latter seem

42. Com (87) 715, 1988.

to be that marketing restrictions, such as advertising regulation or requiring the provision of information, may be imposed on a bank seeking to open cheque accounts or ATM terminals in other Member States. There is, however, a grey area between, on the one hand, these marketing rules, and, on the other hand, the rules concerning establishment which clearly come within the prerogative of the home country. What, say, if a Member State sought to limit the charges which could be placed on use of payment cards? If challenged by a bank from another Member State, this might be justified on the grounds of the Second Directive's 'public interest', in that the charges for payment cards would then be the same as for use of cheques (if this were the case). But another approach might be to say that such a restriction could not be justified in terms of art. 19, since the public interest can be protected in other ways, for example making the charges on payment cards and cheques publicly available, so that consumers can choose which to use.

Payment cards

Finally, the Community has taken limited steps in relation to payment cards. The 1985 White Paper on completing the internal market signalled the Commission's intention to define common technical features of the machines used to produce new payment cards, so that they could be identical, and to encourage the conclusion of agreements at European level between banks, traders, producers and consumers on the compatibility of systems, network linkage, user rules, and/or rates of commission.[43] In a communication to the Council in early 1987, the Commission argued strongly for 'card inter-operability', that is that payment instruments should be comparable and the system networks interconnectable. It was important for the Community, said the Commission, that ATM and EFTPOS cards issued in one Member State could be used in the others where similar services were supplied. That depended on co-operation among the various card systems, in particular to achieve technical compatibility, notably through standardisation.[44]

To provide a framework for that co-operation, the Commission proposed various steps. First, a framework Regulation for co-operation between industrial suppliers, principle users,

43. Commission of the European Communities, *Completing the Internal Market, White Paper from the Commission to the European Council*, Luxembourg, 1985, p. 32.
44. See footnote 41.

telecommunication bodies and specialised research institutes. Secondly, a possible directive to consolidate standardisation of micro-circuit cards. Thirdly, co-operation among the various payment systems to ensure inter-operability (but consistently with Community competition policy so that price and conditions were transparent and that there was no unwarranted differentiation between transactions in the home market and those that involve use of cards in another Member State). Fourthly, further study of matters such as supervision of card issuers, the free transmission of payment data, and consumer protection.

The Regulation and suggested directive will not be pursued. The Commission apparently takes the view now that standardisation in this area is difficult to achieve by legal measures. However, in the light of the Commission's communication, it has now made recommendations on a European code of conduct for electronic payment.[45] The code is to govern the relationship between financial institutions, traders and service establishments and consumers. In particular it is designed to ensure fair practice and that payment systems are as inter-operable as possible. The Commission justifies a code as opposed to binding instrument, because 'it is clear that to try now, at Community level, to produce a rigid, detailed definition of the operation systems in the midst of change might result in the establishment of rules that would be rapidly overtaken by developments, even constituting obstacles to electronic development . . .' (Preamble). Like many codes, however, this one is vague in important respects. The code applies to payment transactions carried out by means of a card incorporating a magnetic strip of microcircuit used at an electronic payment terminal, or point-of-sale terminal. It does not cover company specific cards which do not fall within this definition, cards serving purposes other than direct or deferred payment, payments by cheque with bank card guarantees, and payments by cards using mechanical processes (invoice slips).

As regards contracts between issuers and traders and issuers and consumers, the code says that they should be in writing and the result of prior application. Presumably the latter is directed, in part, at the unsolicited mailing of payment cards. The contract must set out in detail the conditions of the agreement, which shall be freely negotiable and clearly stipulated in the contract. The standard form of contracts used by banks are hardly 'freely negotiated', although it would be a surprising result if the code

45. Commission Recommendation of 8 December 1987 on a European Code relating to Electronic Payment (87/598/EEC), OJ No. L365/72, 24 December 1987.

were intended to be directed against these. More specifically, the code says that any scale of charges must be determined in a transparent manner, taking account of the actual costs and risks and without any restriction on competition. Moreover, conditions specific to termination of the contract must be stated and brought to the notice of the parties prior to the contract being concluded. Since the code mentions only the termination clause in this context, it would seem that at the least it requires the 'red hand' treatment in any conditions of use.[46]

The code then says that by the date by which the internal market must be complete (that is, the 31 December 1992), inter-operability in the Community 'shall be full and complete, so that traders and consumers can join the network[s] or contract with the issuer[s] of their choice with each terminal being able to process all cards'.[47] Inter-operability is defined as a state of affairs whereby cards issued in one Member State and/or belonging to a given card system can be used in other Member States and/or in the networks installed by other systems. This requires that the cards and readers used in the various systems must be technologically compatible and that systems must be opened up by means of reciprocity agreements. Since, under the code, inter-operability must be full and complete, and each terminal must be able to process all cards, the code seems to be saying that any card covered by the code must be usable in every ATM or EFTPOS in the Community. It is unrealistic to expect that by 1992 the holder of, say, a UK issued card will be able to use it in any terminal in Greece. The code is not, of course, legally enforceable.

The code says that terminals are required to register, control and transmit payments. Presumably transmission does not have to be on-line, although this is the trend of the technology. The code continues that traders must be able, if they wish, to install a single, multi-card terminal. Moreover, they must be free to choose which point-of-sale terminal they will install. Of course it must be usable on an inter-operable basis. Later the code says that contracts must not restrict a trader's freedom of operation or freedom to compete. Under 'fair access to the system', it also says that irrespective of their economic size, all service establishments must be allowed fair access to the system of electronic payment,

46. 'Some clauses which I have seen would need to be printed in red ink on the face of the document with a red hand pointing to it before the notice could be held to be sufficient': *Spurling Ltd* v *Bradshaw* [1956] 2 All ER 121, 125; approved in *Interfoto Ltd* v *Stiletto Ltd* [1988] 1 All ER 348, 351, 355.

47. Clause III 2.

although it adds the unhelpful qualification that a trader may be refused access for legitimate reasons only, without attempting to define these. In addition, the code says that there must be no unwarranted difference in the remuneration for services concerning transactions within one Member State, and the remuneration for the same services concerning transactions with other Community countries. Finally, in its supplementary provision the code says that traders must display in a fully-visible manner, the signs of the companies to which they are affiliated, and must accept those cards. Two supplementary provisions on the relations between issuers and traders are first, that there must be no exclusive trading clauses requiring the trader to operate only the one system; and secondly that compulsory provisions in trader-issuer contracts must be limited strictly to technical requirements for ensuring the system functions properly.

The code contains two important principles under the heading 'data protection and security'. First, it says that payments 'are irreversible. An order given by means of a payment card shall be irrevocable and may not be countermanded.'[48] The code purports thereby to overcome the difficult question of the reversibility of payments. The code also says that information transmitted through a payment system must not in any circumstances breach the protection of privacy. Specifically, '[i]t shall be strictly limited to that normally laid down for transfers and cheques'.[49] The date, the payee, the amount and the payor's account are all that are normally identifiable from a cheque, although in a wire transfer the time of payment may be added. Other than what can be inferred from the name of the payee, no information is transferred about the nature of the transaction.

To further inter-operability, the European Council for Payment Systems – a private organisation, with no executive powers, comprising bank representatives from a large number of European countries – adopted a 'European Accord For Bank Card Usage' in 1987.[50] The objectives of the Accord for reciprocity are to improve the services provided to bank customers travelling in Europe, to develop co-operation between the various European banks and financial institutions, particularly the rationalisation of technological developments, to reduce the cost of these exchanges

48. Clause III 4(a).
49. Clause III 4(b).
50. There is some discussion of the Accord in J. Mitchell, *Electronic Banking and the Consumer – The European Dimension*, London, Policy Studies Institute, 1988, pp. 43–7.

through the increasing use of automatic processing and transmission procedures, and to develop co-ordinated and effective security measures. The Accord purports to cover paper-based cash withdrawals at bank counters and payments for goods and services, as well as electronic withdrawals and payment both at bank counters and ATMs.

The Accord has a narrower conception of the principle of reciprocity as compared with the idea of inter-operability in the EEC's code. Under it, banks are free to decide which payment instruments they will issue for cross-border usage. It is only cards which member banks wish to give a European service which are covered, rather than 'all' cards, as under the code. Moreover, it is a matter for the banks to organise acceptance of such cards as is satisfactory to them. The holders of these cards must not then suffer any discrimination, and must be able to take advantage of the European cross-border services which their card provides at the fee agreed. Retailers, which have been contracted with participating banks for the purposes of extending European co-operation in accordance with the agreement, must accept all cards for payment which have been nominated for use in the retail sector.

Issuing banks on the one hand, and retailers, banks and encashing banks on the other, undertake certain responsibilities. For example, the former must make information available for the effective use of cheque guarantee cards (for example, blacklists); be able to issue authorisation, when required, at all times; settle payments; pay the service fees laid down under the agreement; assume the risk involved in the issuing of cards; and provide the information necessary to combat fraud.

The Accord recognises that reciprocity depends on the level of service provided. Consequently, all participants in the Accord agreed to offer cash withdrawal facilities, in particular through all those automatic teller machines and automatic cash dispensers which meet the minimum technical and security requirements set out in the Accord. A vaguer undertaking is that participants agree to achieve 'a minimum level of acceptance' in the retail network within a given period of time. The Accord proposes reviews of progress and foreshadows the payment of compensation by countries not achieving agreed levels.

The Accord contains various provisions about technical reciprocity. As a minimum requirement, all automated terminal machines and cash dispensers providing the European cross-border service must have the capacity to link on-line to the issuer or the issuer's delegated authorisation centre. It is the right of the card issuing bank to state the network through which it wishes to receive traffic. Recognition symbols are apparently not mandatory on all cards, but must be used as agreed. They must be displayed on automated teller machines and cash dispensers (as soon as the machines are able to provide the inter-European card withdrawal service), at branches available for cash withdrawals, and by retailers. Parties to the Accord agree to undertake various measures in relation to security and the prevention of fraud. As would be expected there are detailed provisions for tariffs and fees. Co-ordination of clearing and settlement is left vague; it is matter of joint responsibility, where common regulations are contemplated, but to be determined by participants 'in the light of ongoing developments'.[51]

At the time of writing, the Accord has not achieved wide acceptance amongst existing card issuers. Apparently it is felt that it is too restrictive for individual card issuers, and that in any event it might be in breach of some domestic competition laws. Visa, on the one hand, and Access/Eurocard/Mastercard on the other have reached agreement on the inter-operability of automated teller machines. (Inter-operability for EFTPOS will follow later.) The agreement allows cardholders to withdraw cash from each other's ATMs.

In addition to the code on inter-operability, the Commission is pursuing a separate consumer protection initiative in relation to electronic funds transfer. The code itself contains various provisions touching on card users,[52] but the justification for a separate initiative is that national rules are highly divergent and if no action is taken at the Community level, the divergence will persist, if not increase. This will hamper the development of international and inter-operable payment systems. The initiative takes the form of a recommendation addressed to payment card users, especially banks, establishing minimum rules for the protection of consumers in the Community.[53]

Under the recommendation, card issuers must provide full, written terms of contract, expressed in easily understood language. The onus is on them in any dispute with cardholders. The card issuer is to be liable for the consequences for defects in, or a failure in the operation of, the system. (The liability might be shared by

51. Section 2, ch. 2.3(a).

52. A supplementary provision says that cardholders must take all reasonable precautions to ensure the safety of the card issued and must observe the special conditions regarding loss or theft in the contract signed (IV. 2).

53. 'Commission Recommendation concerning payment cards, and in particular the relationship between cardholder and card issuer', OJ L317/55, 24 November 1988.

others such as the retailer or the network assembler.) Cardholders should be liable for damages arising from the loss of a card until the consumer notifies the issuer. That liability may not exceed the equivalent of 150 ECUs unless consumers have committed an act of extreme negligence or behaved fraudulently. Card issuers must provide a means whereby their customer may at any time notify the loss, theft, or copying of their card. Cardholders must be provided with a written record of each transaction.

Recommendations do not, of course, have any direct binding force under the Treaty.[54] The legal justification for a recommendation rather than a binding instrument is that the latter is not essential to the completion of the internal market to 1992. It is said that the consumer has a choice of payment systems within any one Member State, and uniform conditions throughout the Community for all cards is not necessary to realise the internal market. Of course it may be that there are independent reasons for a Community consumer protection measure separate from the steps necessary for the completion of the internal market by 1992. The Commission has said that if within a year of the Recommendation the banks have not embodied the suggested terms in their contracts with consumers, it will consider a binding initiative. In any event, under some systems of domestic law, the Community Recommendation might be admissible as a matter of law to show good custom and practice.[55]

CONCLUSION

There are a number of common problems thrown up by payment and clearing systems, including the European systems discussed in this chapter. Their resolution will occur, if at all, mainly within Member States. Developments at the international level, such as the work of the United Nations Commission on International Trade Law (UNCITRAL) on electronic payment systems, may influence the steps taken by Member States.[56] Community law may also have a role, and it is to this that these final remarks are addressed.

54. Article 14. They are binding as to aims but not as to methods.
55. See R. Cranston, *Consumers and the Law*, 2nd ed., London, Weidenfeld & Nicolson, 1985, p. 37.
56. UNCITRAL is proceeding with its 'Model Rules on Electronic Funds Transfers'. See also its *Legal Guide on Electronic Funds Transfers*, UN. A/CN. 9. SER. B/1, 1987. There is also the work in the United States on Draft Article 4A of the Uniform Commercial Code: for example, B. Geva, 'The Evolving Law of Payment by Wire Transfer – An outsider's view of Draft UCC Article 4A' (1988) 14 *Can. Bus. LJ* 186.

Access on the part of banks to payment and clearing systems has been a matter of some controversy. With some clearing systems, for example, existing members have taken the view that open access is unfair since they have invested the money and effort in establishing them. But there are larger issues as well, in broad terms the operational and financial integrity of the system. Compliance with the rules of the system, such as those about the timetable and the accuracy of work, is just one aspect.[57] Another is the extent to which members or any lender of last resort can be exposed if one member is unable to meet a debit position at the end of the clearing day.[58]

The competition law of the Community is relevant to the question of access. The bank of a Member State denied access to the payment and clearing system in another state, or to that of a more general European system, could argue that this is in breach of art. 85. The outcome will be a matter of assessing whether the rules of the payment and clearing system are designed to exclude potential competitors, whether they can be justified because the applicant lacks the standing to guarantee the operational and financial integrity of the system, and so on.

The Community probably has less to say about the actual operation of payment and clearing systems. The contractual relationships outlined above will continue to be a matter mainly of domestic law. It will thus be a matter of individual contract, or the general law, when payment is final or is irrevocable – issues which have caused considerable discussion among lawyers.[59] The Community would seem to have no interest in whether customers contractually agree not to countermand Eurocheques, or whether a particular domestic law regards payment by credit card, and it would also seem by debit card, as being irrevocable at the time when the card is used.[60]

Even here, however, the Community has demonstrated an interest. For example, as regards revocability, the consumer protection initiative on payment cards recommends that the terms of the contract between card issuer and holder specify

57. See Association for Payment Clearing Services, *Principles for Participation in the Payment Clearing Services*, London, 1987.

58. For example, Associations of Reserve City Bankers, *Report of the Working Group of the Association of Reserve City Bankers on Book-Entry Daylight Overdrafts*, New York, 1986.

59. For example, R. Goode, *Payment Obligations in Commercial and Financial Transactions*, London, Sweet & Maxwell, 1983, ch. 4.

60. Cf. *In re Charge Card Services Ltd* [1988] 3 WLR 764.

— whether the debiting or crediting of operations will be instantaneous and, if not, the period of time within which this will be done;
— for those operations which lead to invoicing of the contracting cardholder, the period of time within which this will be done.

Moreover, it would seem that ultimately the Community must have a more direct involvement in the operation of the ECU clearing system, in addition to the European Investment Bank's membership of the ECU Banking Association. Since 1981, the ECU has been the sole official unit of account of the EEC, and the ECU is used as a means of settlement between monetary authorities of the European Community. After 1992, all EEC citizens will have the right to open ECU enominated accounts. Just as central banks have an interest in the clearing of their own national currency, even if this involves two foreign banks, so it would seem that the Community must ultimately take a greater formal interest in the operational and financial integrity of the ECU clearing system.

It is in the area of consumer access and use of payment systems that the Commission will have its greatest impact. As has been seen, the Commission's notion of inter-operability is ill-defined. Nonetheless, if the Commission achieves nothing more than technical standardisation, the potential for consumer access to payment systems is improved considerably. At this stage, the Commission has not attempted to regulate directly the terms and conditions on which payment cards are issued. However, the terms and conditions of some cards in Europe are inconsistent with the Commission's Recommendation on the matter, and it may be that a Community directive will ultimately be necessary.

APPENDIX

Proposal for a Second Council Directive on the coordination of laws, regulations and administrative provisions relating to the taking-up and pursuit of the business of credit institutions and amending Directive 77/780/EEC

COM(87) 715 final

(Submitted by the Commission to the Council on 23 February 1988)
(88/C 84/01)

THE COUNCIL OF THE EUROPEAN COMMUNITIES

Having regard to the Treaty establishing the European Economic Community, and in particular the third sentence of Article 57(2) thereof,

Having regard to the proposal from the Commission,

In co-operation with the European Parliament,

Having regard to the opinion of the Economic and Social Committee,

Whereas this Directive is to constitute an instrument which is essential for achieving the internal market, a course determined by the Single European Act and set out in timetable form in the Commission's *White Paper*, from the point of view of both the freedom of establishment and the freedom to provide financial services, in the field of credit institutions;

Whereas the approach which has been adopted is to achieve only the essential harmonisation necessary and sufficient to secure mutual recognition of authorisation and of supervisory systems, thus enabling the application of the principle of home country control and the granting of a single licence recognised throughout the Community;

Whereas, in this context, this Directive can be implemented only simultaneously with specific Community legislation dealing with the harmonisation of technical matters relating to own funds, and a solvency ratio;

Whereas, moreover, work to harmonise the conditions relating to the reorganisation and winding-up of credit institutions is also being undertaken;

Whereas harmonisation will also have to be undertaken for the treatment of liquidity, market, interest rate and foreign exchange rate risks run by credit institutions;

Whereas the home Member State may establish stricter standards than those laid down in Articles 3, 4, 9, 10 and 14 in relation to credit institutions authorised by its competent authorities;

Whereas responsibility for the financial soundness of a credit institution, and in particular for its solvency, will rest with the competent authorities of its home Member State and whereas the host country authorities retain responsibility for matters relating to liquidity and the implementation of monetary policy; whereas supervision of market risk should be the subject of close co-operation between the competent authorities of the home and host countries;

Whereas this Directive will join the body of Community legislation already enacted in particular Council Directive 77/780/EEC on the coordination of banking legislation[1], as last amended by Directive 86/524/EEC[2], Council Directive 83/350/EEC on supervision on a consolidated basis[3], and Council Directive 86/635/EEC on the annual and consolidated accounts of banks and other financial institutions[4]; whereas, moreover, the harmonization of certain financial and investment services is undertaken, where the need exists, in specific Community instruments, notably with the intention of protecting consumers and investors;

Whereas the Commission has adopted recommendations on large exposures [87/62/EEC[5]] and on deposit guarantee schemes [87/63/EEC[6]];

Whereas the chosen approach permits, by virtue of mutual recognition, credit institutions authorised in their home Member States freely to undertake, throughout the Community, all the activities shown in the annexed list either by the establishment of branches or by supplying services;

Whereas, as a result, the host Member State can, in relation to the exercise of the right of establishment and the freedom to provide services, require adherence to specific provisions of its own

1. OJ No L 322, 17. 12. 1977, p. 30.
2. OJ No L 309, 4. 11. 1986, p. 15.
3. OJ No L 193, 18. 7. 1983, p. 18.
4. OJ No L 372, 31. 12. 1986, p. 1.
5. OJ No L 33, 4. 2. 1987, p. 10.
6. OJ No L 33, 4. 2. 1987, p. 16.

laws or national regulations on the part of institutions not authorised as credit institutions in their home Member State and with regard to activities not mentioned in the list, provided that, on the one hand, such provisions are compatible with Community law and seek to protect the public good and that, on the other, such institutions or such activities are not subject to equivalent legislation or regulation in their home Member State;

Whereas it is appropriate to extend the benefits of mutual recognition to the activities mentioned in the annexed list when they are undertaken by financial institutions which are subsidiaries of credit institutions, provided that such subsidiaries are included in the consolidated supervision of their parent undertakings and meet certain strict conditions;

Whereas the undertaking of activities which do not appear in the list shall continue to benefit from the rights of establishment and freedom to supply services under the general provisions of the Treaty;

Whereas the Member States should ensure that there are no obstacles to the activities benefiting from mutual recognition being undertaken using the financial techniques of the home Member State, as long as the latter are not in violation of the legal provisions governing the public good in the host Member State;

Whereas the abolition of the authorisation requirement with respect to branches of Community credit institutions, once the harmonisation in progress has been completed, necessitates the abolition of endowment capital; whereas Article 5(2) constitutes a first transitional step in this direction;

Whereas there is an intimate link between the objective of this Directive and the liberalisation of capital movements being achieved by other Community legislation; whereas in any case the measures regarding the liberalisation of banking activities should be in harmony with the measures regarding the liberalisation of capital movements; whereas in the event that the Member States may invoke by virtue of Council Directive .../.../EEC safeguard clauses in respect of the movement of capital, they may suspend the provision of banking services to the extent necessary to comply with abovementioned safeguard clauses;

Whereas the procedures established in Directive 77/780/EEC, notably in relation to the authorisation of branches of credit institutions authorised in third countries, should continue to apply to such institutions; whereas those branches will not benefit from the freedom to supply services under the second paragraph of Article 59 of the Treaty; whereas 'however' requests for authorisation or for the acquisition of a participation from institutions governed by the laws of a third country are subject to a procedure intended to ensure that Community institutions are granted reciprocal treatment in the third countries in question;

Whereas the smooth running of the internal market in banking will require, in addition to common legislative standards, close and regular co-operation between the competent authorities of the Member States; whereas in the case of problems concerning credit institutions the Contact Committee of bank supervisors of the Member States, referred to in the final recital of Directive 77/780/EEC, remains the appropriate forum for discussion and consultation; whereas that Committee is also the body best suited to deal with the reciprocal flows of information covered in Articles 6 and 7;

Whereas, at all events, that procedure does not replace the bilateral collaboration and co-operation established by Article 7 of Directive 77/780/EEC; whereas, in that context, the competent host country authorities can continue, either on their own initiative or following the initiative of the competent home country authorities, to verify that the activities of a credit institution established on their territory are in conformity with the relevant laws, with the principles of sound administrative and accounting procedures and adequate internal control;

Whereas it is necessary, in order to facilitate the achievement of the objectives of this Directive and to take account of the rapid development of national and international financial markets, to introduce a procedure for adaptation of certain technical features; whereas, because of the important and sensitive nature of that adaptation, procedure III, type (a), as defined in Article 2 of Council Decision 87/373/EEC[7], is the most appropriate,

HAS ADOPTED THIS DIRECTIVE:

TITLE 1

Definitions and scope

Article 1

For the purposes of this Directive:

— 'credit institution' is defined in accordance with the first indent of Article 1 of Directive 77/780/EEC,

7. OJ No L 197, 18. 7. 1987, p. 33.

— 'authorisation' is defined in accordance with the second indent of Article 1 of Directive 77/780/EEC,

— 'branch' is defined in accordance with the third indent of Article 1 of Directive 77/780/EEC,

— 'own funds' is defined in accordance with Council Directive .../.../EEC,

— 'competent authorities' is defined in accordance with Article 1 of Directive 83/350/EEC,

— 'financial institution' is defined in accordance with Article 1 of Directive 83/350/EEC,

— 'home Member State' means the Member State where a credit institution is authorised in accordance with Article 3 of Directive 77/780/EEC,

— 'host Member State' means the Member State where a credit institution has a branch or into which it supplies services,

— 'qualified participation' means a holding, direct or indirect, in an undertaking which represents 10% or more of the capital or of the voting rights or which enables the exercise of a significant influence within the meaning of Article 33 of Council Directive 83/349/EEC[8],

— 'initial capital' means paid-up capital or items of a similar nature according to the national legislation of the home Member State,

— 'parent undertaking' is defined in accordance with Article 1 of Directive 83/349/EEC,

— 'subsidiary' means a subsidiary undertaking in accordance with Article 1 of Directive 83/349/EEC.

Article 2

1. This Directive shall apply to all credit institutions.

8. OJ No L 193, 18. 7. 1983, p. 1.

2. It shall not apply to the institutions exempted under Directive 77/780/EEC and listed in Article 2(2) thereof.

3. The credit institutions which, as defined in Article 2(4)(a) of Directive 77/780/EEC, are affiliated to a central body in the same Member State may be exempted from the provisions of Articles 3, 8, and 10 of this Directive provided that, without prejudice to the application of those provisions to the central body, the whole - constituted by the central body and its affiliated institutions - must be the subject of consolidated supervision with regard to the abovementioned provisions.

In cases of exemption, Articles 5 and 16 to 19 shall apply to the whole, as constituted by the central body and its affiliated institutions.

TITLE II

Harmonisation of authorisation conditions

Article 3

1. The competent authorities shall not grant authorisation in cases where initial capital is less than five million ECU.

2. Member States may propose that initial capital be fixed at an amount lower than that provided for in paragraph 1 in the case of institutions whose scope of authorised business is restricted by law or statute. They shall notify the Commission of the institutions concerned and the amounts proposed within six months of the adoption of this Directive. The Commission shall adopt the list of categories of institutions concerned and the relevant initial capital requirements, according to the procedure laid down in Article 20.

Article 4

Competent authorities shall not grant authorisation permitting the taking-up of the business of a credit institution before they have been informed of the identity of shareholders or members, whether direct or indirect, be they physical or legal persons, holding a qualified participation and of the amount of such participations. The competent authorities shall appraise the suitability of the abovementioned shareholders of members.

Article 5

1. Host Member States may no longer require, as provided for in Article 4 of Directive 77/780/EEC, authorisation for branches of credit institutions authorised in other Member States. The establishment and supervision of such branches shall be subject to the provisions laid down in Articles 17 and 19 of this Directive.

2. Until the entry into force of the provisions in implementation of paragraph 1, host Member States may not require, as a condition for authorisation to be granted to branches of credit institutions authorised in other Member States, an initial endowment capital greater than 50% of the initial capital required by national rules for authorisation to be granted to a credit institution of the same nature.

3. Credit institutions shall recover the free use of the funds no longer required as a consequence of the provisions of paragraphs 1 and 2.

Article 6

In the following cases there must be prior consultation with the competent authorities of the other Member State involved:

— the authorisation of a subsidiary of a credit institution authorised in another Member State,

— the authorisation of a subsidiary of the parent undertaking of a credit institution authorised in another Member State,

— the authorisation of an undertaking controlled by persons, whether physical or legal, who control a credit institution authorised in another Member State.

Article 7

1. Requests for authorisation of a subsidiary whose parent undertaking is governed by the laws of a third country or the acquisition of a participation therein as provided for in paragraph 3 shall be subject to the procedure laid down in this Article.

2. The competent authorities of the relevant Member State

shall inform the competent authorities of the other Member States and the Commission of the request for authorisation.

3. In the same manner, when informed, according to the provisions of Article 9, that an undertaking governed by the laws of a third country is considering the acquisition of a participation in a credit institution such that the latter would become its subsidiary, the competent authorities of the relevant Member State shall inform the competent authorities of the other Member States and the Commission.

4. The competent authorities of the Member State concerned must suspend their decision regarding requests as referred to in paragraphs 2 and 3 until the procedure provided for in paragraphs 5 and 6 is completed.

5. The Commission shall, within three months of receiving the information provided for in paragraphs 2 and 3, examine whether all credit institutions of the Community enjoy reciprocal treatment, in particular regarding the establishment of subsidiaries or the acqusition of participations in credit institutions in the third country in question.

6. If the Commission finds that reciprocity is not ensured it may extend suspension of the decision referred to in paragraph 4, using the procedure provided for in Article 20.

7. The Commission shall present suitable proposals to the Council with a view to achieving reciprocity with the third country in question.

TITLE III

Harmonisation of conditions relating to the pursuit of the business of credit institutions

Article 8

1. The own funds of credit institutions must not fall below the initial capital required when they were authorised. In appropriate circumstances, the competent authorities may allow an institution a certain limited period in which to restore its own funds to the agreed minimum.

2. The own funds of credit institutions in existence at the time of the date of implementation of this Directive must by 31 December 1996 at the latest be at least equal to the level of initial capital stipulated in Article 3.

Article 9

1. Member States shall require any physical or legal person, who is considering the direct or indirect acquisition of a qualified participation in a credit institution, to first inform the competent authorities, telling them of the size of the intended participation. The abovementioned persons must similarly inform the competent authorities if they propose to increase their qualified participation such that the credit institution would become a subsidiary. The competent authorities shall assess the suitability of the abovementioned persons.

2. Credit institutions shall each year furnish the competent authorities with the names of major shareholders and members as referred to in paragraph 1 and the size of their qualified participations, in accordance with the names registered at the annual general meeting of shareholders and members or in accordance with information received as a result of compliance with the regulations relating to companies quoted on stock exchanges.

3. Member States shall require that in cases where the persons referred to in paragraph 1 exercise their influence in a way which is likely to be to the detriment of the prudent and sound management of the banking activities of the institution, the competent authorities shall take appropriate measures to bring such a situation to an end. Such measures may consist in particular in injunctions, sanctions against directors and managers, or the suspension of voting rights in respect of the shares held by the shareholders or members in questions.

Article 10

1. A credit institution shall not hold a qualified participation of an amount greater than 10% of its own funds in an undertaking which is neither a credit institution, nor a financial institution, nor an undertaking pursuing an activity as defined in Article 43(2)(f) of Directive 86/635/EEC.

2. The total amount of qualified participations in undertakings other than credit institutions, financial institutions or undertakings pursuing an activity as defined in Article 43(2)(f) of Directive 86/635/EEC shall not exceed 50% of the own funds of the credit institution.

3. Shares held temporarily during a financial rescue or restructuring operation or during the normal course of the underwriting process or in an institution's own name on behalf of others shall not be included among qualified participants for the purposes of calculating the limits laid down in paragraphs 1 and 2. Shares not having the character of financial fixed assets as defined in Article 35(2) of Directive 86/635/EEC shall never be included.

4. The limits laid down in paragraphs 1 and 2 may be exceeded in exceptional circumstances. However, in such cases, the competent authorities shall require the credit institution either to increase the volume of own funds or take other remedial measures.

5. Compliance with the limits laid down in paragraphs 1 and 2 shall be ensured by means of supervision on a consolidated basis in accordance with the provisions of Directive 83/350/EEC.

6. Member States need not apply the limits laid down in paragraphs 1 and 2 if they provide that the qualified participations in question are to be deducted when calculating the own funds of a credit institution.

Article 11

1. The competent authorities of the home Member State shall ensure the existence within each credit institution of sound administrative and accounting procedures and adequate internal control mechanisms.

2. The competent authorities shall also ensure that such procedures and mechanisms exist in credit institutions included in the scope of consolidated supervision provided for in Directive 83/350/EEC.

Article 12

1. In Article 7(1) of Directive 77/780/EEC, the end of the second sentence is hereby replaced by the following: 'and all information likely to facilitate the monitoring of such institutions, in particular with regard to liquidity, solvency, control of large exposures, administrative and accounting procedures and mechanisms of internal control'.

2. Host Member States shall retain primary responsibility for the supervision of the liquidity of credit institutions until further co-ordination. Without prejudice to the measures necessary for the reinforcement of the European Monetary System, host Member States shall retain complete responsibility for the measures resulting from the implementation of monetary policy. These measures shall not embody discriminatory or restrictive treatment based on the fact that the credit institution is authorised in another Member State.

3. Until further co-ordination of the risks arising out of open positions, the competent authorities of host Member States may take the necessary measures to require credit institutions authorised in other Member States to make sufficient provision against market risk in respect of operations on securities markets in their territory. They shall co-operate for this purpose with the competent authorities of home Member States.

Article 13

1. Host Member States shall ensure that, where a credit institution authorised in another Member State conducts its business there through a branch, the competent authorities of the home Member State are able, after having first informed the competent authorities of the host Member State, to carry out themselves on-the-spot verification of the information referred to in Article 7(1) of Directive 77/780/EEC.

2. The competent authorities of the home Member State may equally have recourse to one of the verification procedures for branches laid down in Article 5(4) of Directive 83/350/EEC, other than that referred to in paragraph 1.

3. This Article shall not affect the right of the competent authorities of the host Member State to carry out on-the-spot

verification of branches established in their territory in the discharge of their responsibilities under this Directive.

Article 14

Article 12 of Directive 77/780/EEC is hereby replaced by the following text, paragraph 2 of which also applies to exchanges of information between competent authorities provided for in this Directive:

'*Article 12*

1. Member States shall ensure that all persons now or in the past employed by the competent authorities, as well as auditors or experts acting on behalf of the competent authorities, are bound by the obligation of professional secrecy. This means that any confidential information which they may receive in the course of their duties may not be divulged to any person or authority, without prejudice to cases covered by criminal law.

2. Notwithstanding paragraph 1, the competent authorities of the various Member States shall exchange information in accordance with provisions of this Directive and Council Directive 83/350/EEC[9] as well as of the Annex to Commission recommendation 87/62/EEC[10]. This information shall be subject to the same conditions of professional secrecy as those indicated in paragraph 1.

3. Member States may conclude co-operation agreements, providing for exchanges of information, with the competent authorities of third countries only if the information communicated is subject to guarantees of professional secrecy equivalent to those referred to in this Article.

4. Competent authorities receiving information under paragraph 1 or 2 shall use it only:

— to examine the conditions for the taking-up of the business of credit institutions and to facilitate monitoring, on a non-consolidated or consolidated basis, of the pursuit of such business, especially with regard to the monitoring of liquidity,

9. OJ No L 193, 18. 7. 1983, p. 18.
10. OJ No L 33, 4. 2. 1987, p. 10.

solvency, large exposures, and the administrative and accounting procedures and mechanisms of internal control, or

— when the decisions of the competent authority are the subject of an administrative appeal, or

— in court proceedings initiated pursuant to Article 13.

5. Paragraphs 1 and 4 shall not preclude within a Member State or between Member States:

— where there are several competent authorities in the same Member State, the exchange of information between them,

— the disclosure of information necessary to enable institutions which manage deposit guarantee schemes to exercise their functions,

— the exchange of information between the competent authorities and public authorities responsible for the supervision of other financial institutions and insurance companies,

— the exchange of information between the competent authorities and persons responsible for carrying out statutory audits of the accounts of credit institutions.

The authorities and institutions to which such information is sent shall use it only in the discharge of their supervisory functions. The information received shall fall within the professional secrecy rules by which those authorities and institutions are bound.

6. Notwithstanding paragraph 1, Member States may authorise, by virtue of provisions laid down by law, the disclosure, when it is necessary for reasons of prudential control, of certain information to other departments of their central government administration. Member States shall ensure that information received in accordance with paragraph 2 is not disclosed in such cases, except where there is the explicit consent of the authorities which have communicated the information.

7. Member States shall ensure that the professional secrecy

provisions laid down by this Article shall apply to information given by the competent authorities to persons responsible for carrying out statutory audits of the accounts of credit institutions.

Article 15

Without prejudice to the procedures for withdrawal of authorisations and cases covered by criminal law, Member States shall ensure that their respective competent authorities may adopt, as against credit institutions, or those who effectively control the business of those credit institutions. which breach legislative, regulatory or administrative provisions concerning the control of their businesses or the pursuit of their activities, penalties or measures aimed specifically at ending observed breaches or the causes of such breaches.

TITLE IV

Provisions relating to freedom of establishment and freedom to provide services

Article 16

1. Member States shall ensure that at least the activities set out on the list in the Annex may be pursued in any Member State, in accordance with the provisions of Articles 17 to 19, either by the establishment of a branch or by way of the provision of services, by any credit institution authorised and supervised by the competent authorities of the home Member State, in accordance with the provisions of this Directive, whose authorisation permits the pursuit of such activities.

2. Member States shall also provide that at least the activities set out on the list in the Annex may be pursued in any Member State in accordance with the provisions of Articles 17 to 19, either by the establishment of a branch or by way of the provision of services by any financial institution being a subsidiary of a credit institution, or such a subsidiary belonging to several credit institutions, whose articles of association do not prevent the pursuit of those activities and which meets each of the following conditions:

— the parent undertaking or undertakings are authorised as credit institutions in the Member State by whose law the subsidiary is governed,

— the parent undertaking or undertakings hold 90% or more of the shares in the subsidiary,

— the parent undertaking or undertakings have declared that they jointly and severally guarantee the commitments entered into by the subsidiary,

— the subsidiary is effectively included, in particular for the activities in question, in the consolidated supervision of its parent undertaking, or of each of its parent undertakings, in accordance with Directive 83/350/EEC, notably for the calculation of the solvency ratio, for the control of large exposures and for the purposes of limiting participations in accordance with Article 10 of this Directive.

Conformity with these conditions must be verified by the competent authority of the home Member State and the latter must supply the subsidiary with a certificate of compliance which must form part of the notification envisaged in Articles 17 and 18.

The competent authority of the home Member State must ensure the supervision of the subsidiary in accordance with the provisions of Articles 8(1), 9, 11, 12(2), 13, 14 and 15 of this Directive, as well as those of Article 7(1) of Directive 77/780/EEC.

The provisions mentioned in this paragraph shall be applicable to subsidiaries subject to the necessary modifications. In particular, 'credit institution' should read 'financial institution conforming to the conditions laid down in Article 16(2)', and 'authorisation' as 'articles of association'. In Article 17(2), point (c) should read 'the amount of own funds of the subsidiary financial institution and the consolidated solvency ratio of the credit institution which is the parent undertaking'.

If the financial institutions benefiting from the provisions of this paragraph should cease to meet any of the requisite conditions, the host Member State may bring an end to the pursuit, under the provisions of this Directive, of the activities in question on its territory.

Article 17

1. A credit institution wishing to establish a branch in the territory of another Member State shall give notification thereof to the competent authority of its home Member State.

2. Member States shall require the notification mentioned in

paragraph 1 to be accompanied by the following information from the credit institution wishing to establish a branch in another Member State:

(a) the Member State in whose territory it intends to establish a branch;

(b) a programme of operations setting out *inter alia* the types of business envisaged and the structural organisation of the establishment;

(c) the amount of own funds and the solvency ratio of the credit institution;

(d) the address in the host Member State from which documents may be obtained;

(e) the names of those responsible for controlling the activities of the branch.

3. Unless the competent authority of the home Member State has reason to doubt the adequacy of the organisational structure of the credit institution, taking into account the envisaged operations, it shall, within three months of the notification referred to in paragraph 1, communicate the information mentioned in paragraph 2 to the competent authority of the host Member State.

Where the competent authority of the home Member State refuses to send the information mentioned in paragraph 2 to the competent authority of the host Member State it shall give reasons to the institution concerned within three months of receipt of the notification. This refusal shall be subject to a right of appeal to the courts in the home Member State.

4. Before the branch of the credit institution commences its activities the competent authority of the host Member State shall, within a period of three months following receipt of the information mentioned in paragraph 3, prepare for the supervision of the institution pursuant to Article 19 and if necessary may decide, in the interest of the public good, to prohibit the credit institution from engaging in some of the activities envisaged, where the conditions of authorisation in its home country do not preclude such activities, but those activities are not contained on the list in the Annex.

5. On receipt of notice from the competent authority of the host Member State, or in the event of the expiry of the three-month period referred to in paragraph 4 without receipt of any communication from the latter, the branch may be established and commence business.

6. A credit institution wishing to change any of the matters notified pursuant to paragraph 2 shall give written notice of the proposed change to the competent authorities in the relevant home and host Member States at least one month before making the change. If necessary, those authorities may decide whether it will not be possible, in the interest of the public good, for the credit institution to engage in any additional activities which it may envisage which are not precluded under the conditions of authorisation in its home country and which are not contained in the list in the Annex.

Article 18

1. Any credit institution wishing to exercise the freedom to supply services in the territory of another Member State for the first time shall notify the competent authorities of the home Member State of the activities included on the list in the Annex which it intends to undertake.

2. The competent authorities of the home Member State shall, within one month of receipt of the notification mentioned in paragraph 1, send that notification to the competent authorities of the host Member State.

Article 19

1. Responsibility for the supervision of a credit institution, including supervision of activities undertaken according to the provisions of Article 16, shall rest with the competent authorities of the home Member State.

2. Host Member States may require, for statistical purposes, that all credit institutions having branches in their territories shall report quarterly on their operations in the host Member State to the competent authority of that host Member State.

In order to conform with the responsibilities laid down in Article 12(2) and (3), host Member States may require that branches of credit institutions from other Member States provide the same information as they require from their national credit institutions for that purpose.

3. If the competent authority of the host Member State ascertains that an institution having a branch or providing services in its territory is not complying with the legal provisions in force in that Member State which are justified on the grounds of the public good, or pursuant to the provisions of this Directive on the powers of the host Member State, that authority shall request the institution concerned to put an end to the irregular situation.

4. If the institution concerned fails to take the necessary steps, the competent authority of the host Member State shall inform the home Member State accordingly. The authority of the home Member State shall take, in the shortest time possible, all appropriate measures to ensure that the institution concerned puts an end to the irregular situation. The nature of those measures shall be communicated to the competent authority of the host Member State.

5. If, despite the measures taken by the home Member State pursuant to paragraph 4, or because such measures prove inadequate or are not taken by the Member State in question, the institution persists in violating the legal rules referred to in paragraph 3 in force in the host Member State, the latter State may, after informing the competent authority of the home Member State, take appropriate measures to prevent further irregularities including, insofar as is necessary, the prevention of the initiation of further transactions by that institution within its territory. The Member States shall ensure that within their territory it is possible to serve the legal documents necessary for these measures on credit institutions.

6. Any measure adopted pursuant to paragraphs 3, 4 and 5 involving penalties or restrictions on the provision of services must be properly justified and communicated to the institution concerned. Every such measure shall be subject to a right of appeal to the courts in the Member State whose authorities adopted it.

7. Before following the procedure set out in paragraphs 3, 4 and 5, the competent authorities of the host Member State may, in exceptional circumstances, take measures necessary to protect the interests of depositors, investors and others to whom services are provided. The Commission and the other Member States shall be

informed of such measures in the shortest possible time. In this event the Commission may, after consulting the Member States concerned, decide that the Member State in question shall amend or abolish the measures.

8. In the event of withdrawal of authorisation the competent authority of the host Member State shall be informed and shall take appropriate measures to prevent the institution concerned from undertaking further transactions in its territory.

9. Member States shall inform the Commission of the number of and type of cases in each Member State in which there has been a refusal pursuant to Article 17 or in which measures have been taken in accordance with the provisions of paragraph 5 of this Article. Every two years, the Commission shall submit a report summarising such cases to the Advisory Committee set up under Article 11 of Directive 77/780/EEC.

TITLE V

Final provisions

Article 20

1. Technical amendments to this Directive in the following areas:

— extension of the activities on the list mentioned in Article 16 and set out in the Annex,

— the amount of initial capital laid down in Article 3(1),

— the list of categories of institution referred to in Article 3(2),

— the thresholds set in Article 10,

— the fields in which the competent authorities must exchange information, as enumerated in Article 7(1) of Directive 77/780/EEC,

shall be made according to the procedure set out in paragraph 2.

2. The Commission shall be assisted by a committee composed

of representatives of the Member States and chaired by a representative of the Commission.

The representative of the Commission shall submit to the committee a draft of the measures to be taken. The committee shall deliver its opinion on the draft within a time limit which the chairman may lay down according to the urgency of the matter. The opinion shall be delivered by the majority laid down in Article 148(2) of the Treaty in the case of decisions which the Council is required to adopt on a proposal from the Commission. The votes of the representatives of the Member States in the committee shall be weighted in the manner set out in that Article. The chairman shall not vote.

The Commission shall adopt the measures envisaged if they are in accordance with the opinion of the committee.

If the measures envisaged are not in accordance with the opinion of the committee, or if no opinion is delivered, the Commission shall, without delay, submit to the Council a proposal relating to the measures to be taken. The Council shall act by a qualified majority.

If, on the expiry of a period to be laid down in each act to be adopted by the Council under this paragraph but which may in no case exceed three months from the day of referral to the Council, the Council has not acted, the proposed measures shall be adopted by the Commission.

Article 21

1. Branches which have commenced their activities, in accordance with the provisions in force in the host Member State, before the entry into force of the provisions adopted in implementation of this Directive are presumed to have been subject to the procedures envisaged in Article 17(1) to (5). They shall be governed, from the date of entry into force of the provisions adopted in implementation of this Directive, by the provisions of Articles 16, 17(6) and 19. They shall benefit from the provisions of Article 5(3).

2. Article 18 shall not adversely affect rights acquired before the entry into force of the provisions adopted in implementation of this Directive by credit institutions operating through the supply of services.

Article 22

1. Subject to paragraph 2, Member States shall bring into force the laws, regulations and administrative provisions necessary to comply with this Directive on the later of the two dates laid down for the adoption of measures to comply with the Council Directives on the harmonisation of own funds and solvency ratios of credit institutions and at the latest by 1 January 1993. They shall forthwith inform the Commission thereof.

2. Member States shall adopt the measures necessary to comply with the provisions laid down in Article 5(2) of this Directive by 1 January 1990.

3. Member States shall communicate to the Commission the texts of the main laws, regulations and administrative provisions which they adopt in the field covered by this Directive.

Article 23

This Directive is addressed to the Member States.

ANNEX

Business which is integral to banking and shall be included within the scope of mutual recognition

1. Deposit-taking and other forms of borrowing
2. Lending[11]
3. Financial leasing
4. Money transmission services
5. Issuing and administering means of payment (credit cards, travellers cheques and bankers drafts)

11. Including in particular:
— consumer credit,
— mortgage lending,
— factoring and invoice discounting,
— trade finance (including forfeiting).

6. Guarantees and commitments

7. Trading for own account or for account of the customers in:

    (a) money market instruments (cheques, bills, CDs, etc.)

    (b) foreign exchange

    (c) financial futures and options

    (d) exchange and interest rate instruments

    (e) securities

8. Participation in securities issues and the provision of services related to such issues

9. Money broking

10. Portfolio management and advice

11. Safekeeping of securities

12. Credit reference services

13. Safe custody services

INDEX

Kent County Council Education Committee

INVICTA

COUNTY LIBRARY

09410 3D